THE UNDERGRADUATE ESSAY

The
Undergraduate
Essay

ROBIN S. HARRIS
and
ROBERT L. McDOUGALL

THE BOBBS-MERRILL COMPANY, INC.
A Subsidiary of Howard W. Sams & Co., Inc.
Publishers Indianapolis / New York / Kansas City

ACKNOWLEDGMENTS

THE AUTHORS wish to express their indebtedness to the Spectator Ltd. and to the authors for permission to reprint "A New Disease" by Dr. Ffrangcon Roberts, "The Canadian Dilemma" by Desmond Henn, and "The Abbey's Needs" by John Laird; to Professor A. J. M. Smith of Michigan State University and to the *Queen's Quarterly* for permission to reprint "The Refining Fire" (parts of Professor Smith's essay have been used in M. L. Rosenthal and A. J. M. Smith, *Exploring Poetry*, published by the Macmillan Company, New York); to Peter Winch of the University College of Swansea and to the *Universities Quarterly* for permission to reprint "The Universities and the State"; and to Professor R. S. Knox of University College, University of Toronto, and to J. Douglas Frame, an undergraduate in the same College, for permission to print for the first time the essays which appear under their names.

The Undergraduate Essay was originally prepared for use in the Department of English, University College, University of Toronto. The authors are particularly indebted to two members of this Department, Professor A. S. P. Woodhouse and Professor F. E. L. Priestley, for advice and assistance during the initial stage of planning and in the course of three revisions. Their greatest debt is to Professor Edwin Rhodes, now of Magee University College, Londonderry, whose labours in preparing the first draft were as extensive as their own.

ROBIN S. HARRIS
ROBERT L. McDOUGALL

1959

INTRODUCTION

THE WRITING of essays is not as dramatic a feature of undergraduate life as is the writing of final examinations, but it is quite as characteristic. This should occasion no surprise, since the essay and the examination are variations on a single theme. Both are tests of the student's knowledge and, more important, of his ability to educate himself.

A student's final grade in each of the several courses which constitute his year's work is normally determined by combining the mark obtained at a final examination with his term mark in the subject. The relative weight assigned to examination and to term mark varies from university to university, from department to department, and from year to year; sometimes the two are equated (add the two marks and divide by two), often (particularly in honours courses) the final examination receives the greater emphasis, occasionally (for example, in science courses which emphasize laboratory work) the term mark takes precedence. In all cases, however, the term mark is important, and the student's success—viewing success in the most practical of terms—depends to a considerable extent on the mark achieved *before* he enters the examination hall. The term mark normally incorporates the results of one or two class tests, but in science subjects it is principally based on laboratory reports and in arts subjects on essay assignments. In all subjects in the humanities, in most subjects in the social sciences, and in some subjects in the sciences, the student is assigned two to four essays during the academic year. It is not unusual for an undergraduate to write as many as fifteen essays between October and April.

Since essay assignments vary from subject to subject and, indeed, within the same subject, it is not possible to define the undergraduate essay rigorously. Usually an adjective must be attached: *descriptive, critical, expository, argumentative.* Even the noun varies: *report, research paper, book review, term paper.* The variations, however, are superficial rather than profound. All assignments mentioned have three things in common: they are of a certain length (1,000 to 2,000 words); they require that evidence be presented to support the judgments given; and they are all ultimately judged on the success with which the student is able to demonstrate his knowledge of the subject. The latter two factors remind us of the essential similarity of essay (or laboratory report) and final examination. In the last analysis, the successful examination answer is the one which convinces the examiner that the student knows his work; the only way in which the student can convince the examiner of this is by marshalling evidence from his storehouse of knowledge which is relevant to the question asked. In the examination hall, the student has to state his case briefly and without reference to his sources; in writing his essay, he has as much time to prepare his case as he wishes to devote and as many resources to turn to as he wishes to examine. Inevitably the essay will be the more rigorously judged— but it will be judged according to the same criteria.

It has often been said that the perfect educational situation (the perfect university, if you will) was Mark Hopkins at one end of a log and the student at the other—the professor and student in intimate discussion. The situation is ideal if it can be assumed that the student has spent a good deal of time in the library before he sits down at his end of the log. Human beings seldom attain the ideal. This particular ideal—education through close association of master and apprentice—is in especial jeopardy in the twentieth century. As university enrolments steadily increase, the prospect for close association between professor and student becomes increasingly remote. Classes are large (too large, often, for questions from the floor), professors are much occupied with committee work and administration, students with part-time employment and the thousand demands of life in an industrialized society. An hour which might have been devoted to discussion may now be spent daily by both professor and student in the physical task of going to the university and returning home.

The essay provides the best opportunity to close the gap. For the half-hour required to read and criticize the essay, the professor gives the student his undivided attention. Ideally—and often this is provided for—professor and student meet together to discuss the essay after it has been graded; here is a real meeting of minds. The essay, then, is not a routine exercise, a chore for the student to write, a chore for the professor to read. It is, if properly approached by both parties, education in the truest sense.

II

It is not possible to teach a student to write a good essay. It is possible for a student to learn how to achieve this result. All that the teacher can do is, first, to provide the materials needed for the student to educate himself and, second, to demonstrate a likely approach. We educate ourselves.

The authors of *The Undergraduate Essay* accept these truths as self-evident. In Part I, a collection of seven essays, they provide the materials needed—complete essays which can be analysed with a view to determining the principles underlying the effective essay. Reading these essays, the student can ask himself why each is effective or why it is not, and he can find the answers: he can discover how the essay has been organized, how the paragraphs are linked, how the sentences have been drawn together into logical units called paragraphs, how the choice of word or phrase enables the writer to express the idea with precision and grace, how punctuation can be used to achieve different effects. The kind of analysis required is demonstrated in Part II. Here the authors identify the principles which govern sound planning, effective paragraph and sentence structure, apt diction, and functional punctuation by referring to specific essays, specific paragraphs, and specific sentences included in Part I. The chapter on "Planning," for example, is based on an analysis of the organization of one of the seven essays, Dr. Roberts' "A New Disease." The authors show how "A New Disease" is organized, they identify the principles which Dr. Roberts has followed while writing her essay, and they suggest that these principles are observed in all effective essays. In this chapter the authors have not submitted the other essays of Part I to the same analysis, and it is possible that their generalizations are unsound—one swallow does not make a summer. The authors are thoroughly convinced, however, that their generalizations are valid; they have analysed dozens of effective essays and found that the organization of "A New Disease" is typical. But the student should investigate the matter himself. He should examine the organization of "The Canadian Dilemma" or "The Universities and the State" and find out whether the generalizations are in fact valid. Similarly, he should test the principles proposed in the chapters on Paragraph, Sentence, Diction, and Punctuation by analysing other paragraphs and sentences than those selected by the authors in arguing their case. The ideal reader of this book is the student who reads each of the specimen essays six times—once in connection with each of the first six chapters of Part II.

The final chapter of Part II, "The Conventions of Scholarship," is of a different order than its predecessors. It is informational. It explains the facts of life about scholarly writing, and it gives advice about such practical matters as the physical appearance of the manu- script, the use of sources, and the conventional form of footnotes and bibliography.

Finally, some comments on the essays chosen for inclusion in Part I. "A Study of Hamlet's Soliloquies" is a genuine and unedited undergraduate essay; Mr. Frame was a freshman when he wrote it. Mr. Frame's essay is on a topic drawn from the humanities; "The Canadian Dilemma" and "A New Disease" deal with topics drawn from the social sciences and the sciences respectively. These three essays are approximately 1,500 words in length, the average length of the undergraduate essay. "The Abbey's Needs" (also 1,500 words in length) is included chiefly as a reminder that most essays are arguments; Mr. Laird wants one million pounds sterling, and his essay is an attempt to convince people that this money must be provided. The remaining essays are longer (4,000 to 5,500 words); the increased length provides opportunity for the treatment of more complex material. Peter Winch's "The Universities and the State" is a tightly reasoned argument involving philosophic concepts. Pro- fessor Smith's "Refining Fire" is at once a convincing answer to a most difficult question (Why read poetry?) and a demonstration of how quotations can be used to support an argument. Professor Knox's essay is a fine example of how to handle a great mass of material without loss of control—he refers to no less than thirty-two critics and scholars in his 4,000 word survey.

A comparison of the short with the longer essays will reveal no fundamental difference. The principles which govern Dr. Roberts in the organization of her material also govern Professor Knox in the organization of his. Professor Smith's paragraphs are effective for the same reasons that Mr. Henn's are effective. Mr. Winch's punctua- tion is in accord with that used by Mr. Laird and Mr. Frame. Nor would a difference appear were we to compare the 1,500 word essay with a 10,000 word essay or a 50,000 word book. The principles identified here as those which govern the effective undergraduate essay are precisely the principles which govern effective prose composition in any form.

CONTENTS

Part I

SPECIMEN ESSAYS

A New Disease

By DR. FFRANGCON ROBERTS

FROM TIME TO TIME new diseases make their appearance. Some are attributable to social or scientific progress—to contact with new products of chemical industry or adventure into new physical conditions. In others the origin is obscure. The latest of these is of a particularly distressing kind. It is a form of blindness in both eyes practically confined to premature babies. From its main characteristic, the formation of fibrous or scar tissue behind the lens, it is called retrolental fibroplasia. From this tissue strands extend across the interior of the eyeball to the retina, and these on contracting cause retinal detachment.

In labelling a disease "new" caution is needed. Some diseases are new only in the sense that new methods of diagnosis or treatment bring them to light. The classical example is appendicitis. Others are merely pre-existing diseases separated out from an ill-defined group by better understanding of their nature. Retrolental fibroplasia belongs to neither of these categories. Since the eye, by virtue of its transparency, lends itself uniquely to direct examination by means of the ophthalmoscope, an instrument which has been in use for many years, it is inconceivable that the previous existence of this condition could have been overlooked. It is, without doubt, a new disease.

Although sporadic cases of somewhat similar conditions had been recorded since 1820, it was unknown as a definite disease until 1942, when it was described by an American ophthalmologist. It was first reported in this country [Great Britain] in 1949, and in France and Australia in 1951. Both here and in the United States it has become the commonest cause of blindness in pre-school children. In the United States it accounts for one-third of blindness from all causes. In this country, so far, the proportion is smaller, but in the last few years twenty-two cases have been reported from the Oxford area alone and nineteen have been found in 120 inmates of the Sunshine Homes. The incidence varies directly with the degree of prematurity.

Reprinted from *The Spectator*, Dec. 19, 1952, 837–8.

According to one American series it affects 23 per cent of babies weighing less than 3 lbs. at birth, 7 per cent of those between 3 and 4½ lbs. and 5.5 per cent of those over 4½ lbs. Above 5 lbs. it is rare. All observers agree that the incidence is increasing.

The cause is entirely unknown. The disease is not contagious, nor is it due to social conditions or to any discoverable abnormality or infection of the mother. It is first observed shortly after birth, but whether the process starts before or after birth is disputed. The formation of the fibrous mass must be the end-result of an antecedent process. Anomalies of the blood vessels and persistence of embryonic structures have been described, but whether these are causes or associated disturbances is unknown. In any case, to attribute the disease to them is only to push the explanation one stage further back. Some authorities believe it to be part of a more extensive disorder, finding other congenital manifestations, including mental deficiency, in some of their cases. Such concomitants seem, however, to be rare.

It has been variously attributed to one or other of the hazards, natural or artificial, involved in premature exposure to the rigours of post-natal life—incomplete temperature control, vitamin deficiency and digestive or dietetic failure. Premature exposure to light, which would seem a likely cause, is ruled out since the disease is not prevented by covering up the eyes. Treatment of concomitant anaemia by blood-transfusion is equally unsuccessful. Oxygen deficiency, due to persistence of the foetal type of circulation, has been suggested, but so also has the administration of oxygen in too high concentration. Neither increase nor decrease in the amount of oxygen given has proved effective.

These explanations, apart from being disproved by the failure of the appropriate corrections, neglect the fact that this is a new disease superimposed on a condition which has always been with us. In Switzerland, where the treatment of prematurity has long been of a high standard, it is very rare. Though a disease of prematurity, it is not due to prematurity or to any of the known causes of prematurity. Clearly some new factor is involved. The assertion recently made by a Member of Parliament that it is a result of the Health Service is only partly true. The service, by providing more extended facilities for forms of treatment already in use, merely increases the number of potential victims. On the other hand, the statement recently broadcast by the Minister of Health to the effect that decline in infant-mortality is a measure of improvement in national health requires modification.

Infection, probably by virus, has been suggested, and has some evidence in its favour. It would explain the remarkable geographical variation in incidence which is found not only in different parts of the same country—it is twice as high in Illinois as in New York—but also in different hospitals in the same town. It would also explain the observation that, apart from twin-pregnancies, it has never been seen twice in the same family, a fact which suggests that the mother acquires immunity on the first occasion. It is now well established that an attack during pregnancy of German measles, an infection once considered harmless enough, is liable to result in abnormalities of the offspring. It may well be that in the condition which we are discussing the mother contracts some infection too trifling to be noticed.

For the established disease no cure has been found. Attempts have been made to restore some degree of retinal function by surgical removal, in part at least, of the fibrotic mass. Radiotherapy has been used, so far without success, in the hope of inducing regression. A method which in some ways has a more rational basis is the administration of the substance known as A.C.T.H. (adrenocorticotropic hormone), the recently discovered secretion of the pituitary gland which stimulates the suprarenal gland to produce cortisone, a substance which is known to induce regression of abnormal fibrous tissue. First results were indeterminate, but more recently workers in this country have claimed some success. As in the treatment of other diseases, the assessment of results is rendered difficult by the occasional tendency to spontaneous arrest and regression. The surest way to prevent the disease lies, of course, in preventing prematurity. Meanwhile search for the cause requires, and is indeed engaging, the co-ordinated energies of obstetricians, paediatricians and ophthalmologists. The number of cases seen at any one centre being small, collation of experience is essential, and is being undertaken by the Medical Research Council.

This disease, the serious social implications of which require no emphasis, illustrates many of the difficulties encountered in medical research. It demonstrates the increasing complexity of our concepts of disease-processes, the great width of the investigational net which must be cast, the difficulty in distinguishing cause from effect, and the multiplicity of attempted remedies which, so long as the cause remains a mystery, are no more than empirical. Its almost simultaneous appearance in regions as far apart as Western Europe, America and Australia raises the fundamental problem of the genesis of disease. Finally, it proves, if further proof be needed, the sombre and sobering truth that the environment against which man struggles, so far from being constant and static, is ever changing, ever evolving and dynamic, and that on the chess-board of medical science nature is always one move ahead.

The Canadian Dilemma

By DESMOND E. HENN

SINCE THEY have not as yet been made the recipients of Marshall Aid, it is more than a little surprising to discover that Canadians have reacted quite as violently as any left-wing European to the post-war shift in world power which has made the United States the economically dominant nation of Western civilization. This reaction is especially puzzling to the many people, both in Europe and the United States, who regard Canadians and Americans as virtually indistinguishable. An American businessman who has settled in Canada told me: "If it wasn't for the Customs posts, you could cross from Alberta to Montana, or from Ontario to Michigan, without realizing you were going to a different country. Canadian civilization is modelled on ours, and the two peoples think and act alike."

This is perfectly true, but a great many Canadians fervently wish it were not. Anxious to enjoy the benefits of a standard of living comparable to that of their neighbours, they have discovered, with mingled feelings of surprise and dismay, that the price they must pay for their prosperity is the almost complete extinction of their national identity—a fragile plant that is at present the more tenderly cherished for having so little perceptible existence. This discovery in turn has led many citizens of the Dominion to regard Americans in general—not, it should be emphasized, individual Americans—with a hostility compounded in equal parts of envy and resentment. It may perhaps be worthwhile to enquire to what extent these somewhat ungracious sentiments have any justification in fact.

Canadians have a painfully simple reason for being envious; the fact is that virtually everything requiring an outlay of money, from cigarettes to gasoline, from railroad fares to rents, is cheaper in the United States. Disgruntled Canadians think this phenomenon both unfair, which it is, and inexplicable, which it is not. Were one to consider the Dominion's economic resources alone, there would appear to be no valid reason why its citizens should not enjoy a standard of living comparable to, or higher than, that to be found

Reprinted from *The Spectator*, Feb. 27, 1953, 238-9.

south of the border. The explanation of why this possibility has not been realized is to be found in two additional circumstances: first, Canada is still in the initial stage of a long-term boom, and her population is as yet far too small to make large-scale mass production and nationwide distribution-networks feasible; secondly, and perhaps more important, the Dominion Government has imposed a heavy scheme of taxation in order to finance a welfare programme which many people feel to be more ambitious than a nation of this size can afford without crippling, or at least inhibiting, its development in the immediate future.

Indeed, many Canadians, irked by the cost-of-living disparity between their country and the United States, are inclined to lay the whole blame on meddlesome politicians in Ottawa. The fact that freight tariffs on the Government-supervised railroads have soared to the point where Montreal manufacturers shipping goods to Vancouver now find it cheaper to send them in British tramp-steamers via the Panama Canal, rather than across the continent by rail, is certainly not a healthy sign; and Ottawa must be held to a large extent responsible for favouring a policy of present security at the cost of future expansion.

Canadian resentment of the United States requires a more subtle analysis. Broadly speaking, one may say that no nation can foster among its people a consciousness of national identity unless one at least of the following conditions is fulfilled: the country must be sufficiently small and compact to permit of easy and frequent access to any of its parts; or its inhabitants must be of approximately the same descent, sharing a similar *Weltanschauung* and cherishing a common cultural heritage; or they must be united from without by allegiance to some ideal—whether it be the concept of a national destiny, as in the Third Reich, or simply of an inchoate way of life, as in the United States. The first two requirements are both present in Britain, the second alone in France, the third in America. None of them is to be found in Canada.

The country is at present badly under-populated, and progress in correcting the situation is discouragingly slow. Even in this age of air-travel the gulf in outlook and temperament which separates, for example, Vancouver, Edmonton and Calgary on the one hand from Toronto and Montreal on the other is incomparably greater than the distance between them. The gulf would matter but little were the inhabitants of Canada more or less homogeneous. But this is not the case. Those of English descent now number about 48 per cent of the population, a figure which is decreasing annually, while the French element, having evinced an obdurate and at times bitter refusal to be assimilated, is steadily becoming more numerous. The chances of welding those two disparate elements into a single nation seem very remote unless some magic talisman can be found that will enable people throughout the Dominion to feel that "being a Canadian" has some significance beyond a mere indication of their place of residence. To their unspeakable chagrin, Canadians have as yet been unable to devise anything remotely resembling this ideal; no national dream that is both new and indigenous has taken root on Canadian soil. The result is that the country is occupying its place in the world not as a unified nation but as an uneasy confederation of mutually anti-pathetic racial and religious groups, each of which, rejecting a mere loyalty to the Dominion as being vague and almost meaningless, is turning to the past in search of a more substantial creed to which it can owe allegiance.

Considered against this background, Canadian resentment of the United States becomes, if not forgivable, at any rate understandable. Confronted with the colossus of American civilization continually threatening to reduce their country to the status of a cultural and economic satellite, Canadians realize that they can resist the invasion only by opposing against it a more substantial bulwark than that provided by their timid and half-hearted patriotism. Thus English-Canadians tend to maintain their devotion to the Commonwealth tie, and to the Crown through which it is personified, not—as Americans occasionally assert—out of a perverse and obsolete sentimentality, nor yet, as many people in Britain would like to believe, out of any particular loyalty to the institution of the monarchy, but simply because they consider it the least disagreeable alternative to becoming facsimile Americans.

Similarly, French-Canadians are inclined to bestow on the Church of Rome an authority in secular affairs which might be better exercised in less partial hands were the Dominion in a position to command their confident allegiance. But until the day when Canada comes to stand for its inhabitants as a symbol of some more honourable ideal than a slavish duplication of the American way of life the scars of its present racial and religious disunity will remain unhealed.

It may reasonably be asked: If so many Canadians are envious of the United States, why do they not move there? The answer is that a great many of them—particularly university graduates who feel that the Dominion offers little scope for scientific or academic research—do emigrate, and this is one of the problems which are hindering Canada's development. The even greater number who would like to live south of the border, but who nevertheless remain, do so either because of practical difficulties or because they feel that emigration would be equivalent to deserting to the enemy. Most Canadians devoutly hope that, if they can avoid importing too much popular American culture, they may yet produce a better substitute that will justify their country's existence as a separate nation. But they realize that American magazines, movies, books and now television are already exercising an insidious influence—as they are to a lesser extent in Britain—and that time is short.

One final word: it is not to be inferred from the above that Canada's attitude towards the United States is conditioned solely by a militant hostility. Mankind being what it is, the vast majority of people are quite incapable of forming any conscious and articulate opinion on more than a very few of the questions which affect them, and Canadians are no more gifted in this respect than the citizens of any other land. The possibility of the Dominion rising in arms to defend its cultural integrity must therefore be considered even more remote than the administrative merger so warmly advocated by many Americans a short time ago. But the subconscious antagonism is nonetheless real, and it must inevitably influence relations between the two countries in the years to come.

A Study of Hamlet's Soliloquies

By J. D. FRAME

THE EXPOSITION and rising action of *Hamlet* are based upon Hamlet's state of mind at the outset and his subsequent reaction to the ghost's revelation. Hamlet is to oppose Claudius, and the audience must know his plans, but since he must "hold his tongue"—lest the king discover his suspicion—Hamlet's motives can be disclosed only by means of soliloquy. The soliloquies therefore are basic elements in the play's structure. Much of the appeal of *Hamlet*, however, lies not in excellence of structure but in the character of Hamlet himself. Since the soliloquies are Shakespeare's primary means of delineating Hamlet's character, they assume an importance in the interpretation of the play which overshadows their significance as mere structural devices.

The ability to argue on both sides of a question normally implies only an alert and ingenious mind, but this faculty runs riot once a man loses faith in himself, and, once let slip, seems only to intensify his original feeling of inadequacy. So it is with Hamlet. We must let the Freudians decide whether he is aware of a repressed Oedipus complex. He is certainly disgusted at his mother's "o'erhasty marriage," and perhaps feels obscurely that her sensuality has in some way tainted his own nature. This would give point to John Dover Wilson's emendation of his first soliloquy to "O, that this too too *sullied* flesh would melt" (I, ii, 129). The soliloquy is an agonized statement of the disillusionment caused by his father's death and his mother's marriage, but it also carries overtones of a new, hypercritical attitude toward himself. His own grief, amidst the indifference of the court, forces him to make the first of many comparisons between his own reactions and the reactions of those around him. If his mother's sin has tainted him, he has no right to judge anyone else for indifference to evil. And yet

> How weary, stale, flat and unprofitable
> Seem to me all the uses of this world.   (I, ii, 133–4)

The sands of his values are already shifting. Mankind (as represented by the court) disgusts him, but behind this disgust is an even deeper suspicion of his own motives—perhaps of his own sanity—which destroys his moral equilibrium and his ability to face the difficult decisions soon to be forced upon him.

This theme—the comparison of his own reactions with those of another—is repeated in the soliloquy beginning, "O what a rogue and peasant slave am I!" (II, ii, 525–82). Hamlet sees the player's passion as an implied rebuke for his tardy revenge and, always ready to take the uncharitable view of his own motives, attributes the delay to indifference. Yet indifference is the very fault which, displayed by his mother, had so dismayed him before:

> O God! a beast, that wants discourse of reason,
> Would have mourn'd longer.   (I, ii, 150–1)

He upbraids himself and heaps curses on Claudius in an attempt to lash himself into the fury he thinks he should feel, and then abruptly realizes what he is doing. His self-contempt returns tenfold. His introspection, far from clarifying his problem, ends this time in the obvious conclusion that he is no better than his thoughtless mother. From this point on, Hamlet's powers of decision are trammelled not only in a cloud of brittle logic, but in a deep-seated distrust of his own motives. He admits as much to Horatio, in the play-scene: "My imaginations are as foul/As Vulcan's stithy" (III, ii, 82–3).

When next we see him, Hamlet seems about to come to grips with his problems. We feel that if, like Descartes, he can seize upon some article of faith, no matter how trivial, he may hope for salvation: "To be, or not to be: that is the question" (III, i, 56). He sets aside ethical questions for the moment: "Whether 'tis nobler in the mind to suffer . . . or to take arms" is not the point. The truth is, he decides, that utter extinction is "a consummation devoutly to be wish'd," but who knows whether death means utter extinction? There is always that "dread of something after death"—a dread which

> . . . puzzles the will,
> And makes us rather bear those ills we have
> Than fly to others that we know not of.   (III, i, 78–82)

And at the end of this soliloquy, Hamlet is no nearer his goal. Indeed, the line between good and evil, which was only blurred for him before, has now completely vanished, and he can only ask Ophelia,

"What should such fellows as I do, crawling between earth and heaven?" (III, i, 126–7).

Hamlet's decision to spare Claudius in the prayer-scene seems at first to be based upon the certain knowledge of the life after death that he had so recently questioned: "And now I'll do it: and so he goes to heaven" (III, iii, 74). The opposition of thoughts in these two soliloquies compels us to consider them as two facets of the same idea. Here Hamlet, for once, gets the best of two worlds: if the Christian belief is true, then he will lose nothing by sparing Claudius; on the other hand, if death *does* mean extinction, it is far more fitting to leave Claudius to "grunt and sweat under a weary life" than to send him to his rest. In this case, his decision is merely the obverse of Kent's verdict on Lear's death: "He hates him/That would upon the rack of this rough world/Stretch him out longer" (*King Lear*, V, iii, 314–16).

Hamlet's final soliloquy is almost a repetition of his earlier self-recrimination, this time prompted by the sight of Fortinbras' army

> Exposing what is mortal and unsure
> To all that fortune, death, and danger dare,
> Even for an eggshell. (IV, v, 51–3)

He begins by naming, in his defence, the very faculty that assures his downfall:

> Sure, he that made us with such large discourse,
> Looking before and after, gave us not
> That capability and god-like reason
> To fust in us unused. (IV, v, 36–9)

As before, however, his thoughts gravitate to his ever-present distrust of himself and his motives. He is the victim of

> Some craven scruple
> Of thinking too precisely on the event,
> A thought which, quarter'd, hath but one part wisdom
> And ever three parts coward. . . . (IV, v, 40–3)

His constant questioning has not pierced the veil of doubt that envelops him, but has merely turned a harsher light upon his own fancied inadequacies.

This "declension" of Hamlet, as Polonius would say, from "Seems, madam! nay, it is; I know not 'seems'" (I, ii, 76) to "There is nothing either good or bad, but thinking makes it so" (II, ii, 241–2) takes place in an intellectual atmosphere quite alien to Hamlet's spirit. Claudius and the rest have the advantage over Hamlet precisely because of their slow-wittedness. If Claudius is troubled by his actions, it is through vague promptings of an inarticulate moral sense, which in any case he soon stifles. Polonius is so dull as to drive us to fury, with his "Truly in my youth I suffered much extremity for love: very near this" (II, ii, 188–9). Gertrude cannot understand Hamlet's melancholy, although she knows the cause well enough. Rosencrantz and Guildenstern can see no other reason for Hamlet's state of mind than disappointed ambition, and he does not deign to enlighten them: "Sir, I lack advancement" (III, ii, 328). Hamlet's knowledge that such weak wits are parrying his plans for revenge only increases his self-contempt. He constantly tries to pierce their vegetable-like singleness of purpose with bitter gibes, but even this fails. His open defiance of Claudius goes unnoticed. In the face of Hamlet's "I will in all my best obey you, madam" (I, ii, 120)— obviously intended as a bitter thrust at them both—Claudius offers only, "Why, it is a loving and a fair reply." Hamlet's questioning of Polonius about the cloud shaped like a camel, or a weasel, or a whale, may be read as an attempt to show the old schemer that everything is not so simple as it seems, but this too is a failure. Even the sane and resigned Horatio forces from Hamlet, "There are more things in heaven and earth, Horatio,/Than are dreamt of in your philosophy" (I, v, 159–60).

This study of a man struggling in a mire of doubt created by his own too active brain has made *Hamlet* the most intriguing work in English literature. Hamlet is an image of modern man, cast loose from certainty, trying vainly to find bottom in an ocean of disbelief. The appearance in drama of characters like Hamlet is the sign of man's emergence from the "Age of Faith," and as long as men continue to search for certainty Hamlet will remain, as Coleridge calls him, "the darling of every country in which the literature of England has been fostered."

The Abbey's Needs

By JOHN LAIRD

THE COLLEGIATE CHURCH of St. Peter in Westminster, more familiar to the world still as Westminster Abbey, has been eight hundred and eighty-eight years in the building, and it is not finished yet. Nor will it ever be finished, unless it is blown to bits by a bomb or allowed to fall into decay by apathetic generations. For a building of such age and scale and architectural complexity must survive as a living work of art if it is to survive at all: maintenance is too small a word to describe the endless and annually intensifying battle which must be fought against the forces which attack the fabric everywhere and destroy its weakest parts. That is why one says that the building of the Abbey is not finished yet. Maintenance, repair, restoration, replacement: there is no end to it, and it is in the light of this perpetual effort that one must consider the appeal for a million pounds which is launched today.

The last appeal, thirty-three years ago, brought in £168,000, and this went a little way towards arresting decay. During the war years, however, all but the most urgent work was suspended, and now the battle has clearly become more unequal than ever before. Decay has the upper hand again, and parts of the external stonework are becoming dangerous: there are, for example, two stretches of stone parapet, above the nave and the west side of the south transept, which would certainly have fallen if they had been leaning outward; luckily, they inclined inward and could be shored. There are nineteen items in the category of stonework alone on the Surveyor's list of repairs. To deal with the smallest of them will cost (at present-day prices, which are anything but stable) £2,500, and with the largest, £25,000. It is estimated, in fact, that no less than £100,000 is needed for urgent repairs to the main structure.

The Abbey's doors are closed against the public now, and against the Dean and Chapter too, for that matter, so that the Ministry of Works can make with Byzantine thoroughness its preparations for the great spectacle of Elizabeth II's coronation. It may be thought

Reprinted from *The Spectator*, Jan. 30, 1953, 120.

that, while this is the best of all years in which to make an appeal to
the public's generosity, with the eyes of much of the world turning,
as June draws nearer, towards the Abbey, it is also unfortunate that
the public should be asked for help while the public is locked out of
the building which, more than any other in London perhaps, they
have come in recent years to regard as their own inheritance. That,
however, is another matter, and it is too late now to bring up the
rights and wrongs of closing the Abbey for such a period. Even if
one were still free to wander round the high-roofed interior, one
would not see the cracks and gaps and flaws which demand immediate attention: they are far above the ground and out of sight
for the most part. But in the cloisters there is more than enough
evidence of the disastrous effect of London's poisonous atmosphere
on stone which is not kept clean. The surface of the walls and
vaulting is pocked and scabbed by a black corrosion; any sharp
change in temperature removes another fraction of an inch in flakes
of cheesy stone. This is an offence to the eye, and that is bad; but
the black rot is sinking surely towards the core of the stone, and
that is infinitely worse, for it is the entire structure itself that is being
threatened more ominously every month. Various preservatives have
been tried in the past, but to no avail, and now an immense amount
of work must go to the restoration of the stonework in the cloisters.
This will cost at least £60,000, and when that is done there will
remain the continuous expense involved in keeping the surfaces
clean—for that has been found by experience to be the only sure
preservative against corrosion.

These are obviously urgent matters. But the state of the interior
is hardly less alarming, for this too is beset in every nook and cranny
and projection by the corrosive forces at large in London's atmosphere. Some cleaning had been done before the war, but it came
to a stop in 1939 and nothing has been done since then; the work
that remains will take at least ten years to complete and it will cost
not a penny less than £100,000. Every square inch of surface must
be cleaned by hand and with the greatest delicacy if the work of
mason and sculptor and painter, at present obscured by the thick
crust of grime, is not to be spoiled or destroyed. With care the
intricacies and felicities of mediaeval craftsmen and artists will rise
renewed from the filth which at present both hides and devours
them. Photographs of the small area already cleaned show how

startling is the emergence of beauties of detail formerly hidden, and how the general effect is incomparably enriched. Here again it must be stressed that the cleaning of the interior is required for purposes of preservation even more than beautification, for the dirt is active and malevolent.

Twenty years ago the Surveyor of the Fabric and the Clerk of Works had about forty employees—masons, bricklayers, carpenters, joiners, painters, plumbers and electricians—constantly at work on maintenance; and this force was thought to be too small. Today there are only twenty-one. No matter how hard they work they can never hope to arrest the deterioration of the precious fabric in their charge.

There are other matters calling for attention. For the coronation of George VI the rebuilding of the organ had to be completed as quickly as possible and so it was erected without its great carved oak cases. To encase it will now cost £15,000. The Dean and Chapter wish also to endow the Choir School and give it the financial security which at present it lacks. To produce an annual income of £9,000, the capital sum of £260,000 is required.

The Abbey, like St. George's Chapel, Windsor, and unlike any other church in the country, comes under no external ecclesiastical authority. No Bishop or Archbishop rules over the Abbey. The Sovereign is its "Visitor" and so it has the name of a "Royal Peculiar." Apart from this association with the Crown the Abbey is virtually self-governing. The State contributes not a penny to its upkeep. The total income is £59,200, which is £11,000 less than that needed to ensure solvency for the present. To provide that additional income a capital sum of £314,000 must be found.

And so we arrive at the million pounds of the appeal: £314,000 for the maintenance of the fabric; £330,000 for immediate capital expenditure; £260,000 for the choir school; and £70,000 for future capital expenditure. It may seem a lot to ask, but it is certainly no more than is necessary.

The Universities and the State

By PETER WINCH

A LOT IS SAID these days about the role which the universities play, or ought to play, in society; about the "purpose" or "social function" of a university. Of course not everyone agrees about what that function or purpose is; but I am going to argue that the differences of opinion over this are dwarfed in importance by the differences of opinion between all those who hold that the universities have *some* purpose, whatever they may think it specifically is, and those who hold on the other hand, as I do, that universities have no purpose whatever; who hold, to put the position more accurately, that it does not even make sense to *ask* what the purpose of a university is, since institutions such as universities belong to a category which does not logically permit the predication of a purpose. In fact, the view that there are social purposes which particular institutions serve is self-contradictory, as I hope to be able to show.

As this way of putting it suggests, and as one would anyway expect, ideas about university policy do not stand alone; they go together with ideas about the policies of other institutions and, even more fundamentally, with ideas about what a social institution is, how an institution is related to the rest of society and to other institutions, and what role the institution of the state plays in relation to other institutions and the rest of society. In fact, ideas about university policy rest on a social philosophy; and what I want to argue is that the social philosophy presupposed by the view that institutions ought to fulfil a social purpose is internally incoherent and confused.

Of course, this whole line of approach will irritate and be rejected by many of those against whom I want to direct my arguments. They will say that the situation we are in is not one that calls for "arid logic-chopping" or philosophical hair-splitting; that we are faced with an urgent practical problem: that, namely, of how to train enough technologists to keep this country economically viable and how to adapt the development of the universities so as to serve this central aim. They will say that anyone who tries to discuss university policy

Reprinted from *Universities Quarterly*, XII (Nov. 1957), 14–23.

except in relation to this central fact is simply fiddling while Rome burns. In a way they are right about this; and yet the question is not a simple one of finding the best means towards the given end. The whole distinction between means and ends is inadequate in dealing with questions of this sort. To understand, and make use of, a machine for making collar-studs we do not need to know its history— whether it was constructed by slave-labour or free craftsmen, say; but to understand what, for example, the universities are now involves understanding what they were in the past and *how* they have come to be what they are now. Thus the *conceptions* which lie behind present actions for the development of the universities will form part of the very nature of the universities in, say, twenty years' time. To put the general point in philosophical terms: the distinction between means and ends will not suffice here because a social phenomenon, as opposed to a natural one, is internally and not causally related to the historical process out of which it develops. Being clear about what one is doing in policies for university development involves being clear about the nature of the issues which divide the interested protagonists. "Philosophical hair-splitting" is not an irrelevancy diverting our attention from the real practical issues.

Ideas about the nature of society are not passive. They do not merely attempt to reflect the nature of society as it is, but affect the policies which people advocate; and those policies can bring about a change in the nature of society. A social philosophy can be used to support particular policies even if it is self-contradictory. But if it *is* self-contradictory the policies implemented in its name will not have the effects which the philosophy ascribes to them. This is because a self-contradictory proposition does not succeed in specifying any possible state of affairs; it may purport to do so, but in fact it does not. So if the description of a state of affairs which a policy is designed to bring about contains a contradiction, the policy cannot bring that state of affairs about, since, to express myself somewhat Irishly, no possible state of affairs has actually been described.

Consider a simple analogy. "Squaring the circle" is a self-contradictory idea. A man may be unaware of this and in consequence of his unawareness invent a procedure which he thinks will result in the squaring of the circle. His procedure will, of course, result in *something*; but what it cannot result in is the squaring of the circle, since there is no state of affairs which could possibly correspond to this phrase. Similarly, government or the university authorities may greatly expand the technological departments of the universities and they may make possible the acceptance by the universities of a much larger number of students. They may think that in doing this they are allowing the universities to fulfil their true social purpose by serving the needs of society as a whole. But the idea that the universities have any purpose to fulfil, or that society as a whole has any needs to be served, is self-contradictory. Therefore the policy cannot result in the fulfilling of that purpose or the serving of those needs. Certainly the character of the universities will be changed; but not in the way that the advocates of the policy supposed.

Some of my readers will no doubt take me to be cutting the throats of university workers—to be saying that university work is pointless, not worthwhile, and has no claim on anyone's support. Nothing could be farther from my thoughts. Indeed, I am maintaining that it is only in coming to realize that academic work has no ulterior purpose that one can see that it really has a point. But it would be a mistake to look for the point of academic work *outside* the context of academic work itself.

Perhaps this can best be brought home by pointing out that some things must be worth doing for their own sakes if anything is to be worth doing at all. Those who disagree will probably express their disagreement by saying that the only thing which ultimately makes any activity worth performing is happiness or welfare. At this point I should like to quote a passage from the eighteenth-century Bishop Butler's *Sermons*:

> That all particular appetites and passions are towards *external things themselves*, distinct from the pleasure *arising from them*, is manifested from hence; that there could not be this pleasure were it not for that prior suitableness between the object and the passion: there could be no enjoyment or delight from one thing more than another, from eating food more than from swallowing a stone, if there were not an affection or appetite to one thing more than another.

Butler was speaking about the principles underlying the actions of individuals rather than about the justification of social policies. But his argument applies there equally. His point was that happiness, or pleasure, is something that comes with the attainment of ends that are thought worth attaining, or with the engaging in activities which are thought worth engaging in. If *only* happiness were thought worth attaining, and *no* activity were thought worth engaging in except in so far as it promoted happiness, there could be no happiness. We could not attach any meaning to the notion of happiness. Thus the extreme utilitarian position contradicts itself.

How does this apply to the justification of social policies? A society is made up of many institutions—forms of human activity, such as educational, commercial and religious institutions; and within any given institution there will be differing rival conceptions, with their own traditions, of the right way for the activity in question to be carried on. Consider the conflicting views on what living a Christian life involves in our community, or what should be the proper role of the worker in industry. Again, the present article is intended to foster one view, in opposition to others, of the way the work of the universities should be carried on; it is intended to foster a particular *conception* of the universities. Now it is *within* such forms of activity, and in the context of such conflicts between opposing conceptions of the way they should be developed, that social values, ideas of what is good, arise. A university don, say, will have certain ideas about the direction which his work ought to take and about the conditions under which it is best carried on. Those ideas will be intelligible only in the context of the kind of work he is engaged in. They may not be intelligible to someone whose way of life and work is quite different, to a business man, for example; but that is no reflection at all on their validity.

What I have just been saying is open to one particular possible misinterpretation which I should like to scotch in advance. I have said that within any institution there will be rival conceptions of the way its work should be carried on. That does not mean, however, that all such conceptions are therefore equally valid; since what is in question is an opposition between different *conceptions*, the issue between them is essentially one which can be discussed. Where there is the possibility of discussion there must be standards which can be appealed to; not everybody accepts precisely the same set of standards, but on the other hand the standards which the protagonists of different (for example, educational) movements appeal to do overlap to a considerable extent, and this is what permits discussion and creates the possibility of rational changes in people's views. The process is admirably illustrated in some of Plato's dialogues; in the *Gorgias*, for instance, we find Socrates upholding the importance of disinterested intellectual inquiry as against the Sophist, Gorgias, and his followers, who maintain that intellectual abilities are valuable only in so far as they enable their possessor to "get on" in society.[1] It seems at times in this dialogue as if Socrates and his opponents are just speaking different languages, so different are most of the presuppositions from which they set out. But Socrates is able to discuss with Gorgias because he is able to show that Gorgias holds certain views which are incompatible with the general position he wants to maintain; indeed his very grasp of the conception of "intellectual abilities" is incompatible with his belief that the ultimate criterion of the importance of anything is the ability to "get on."

But to say that policies and values may be discussed and that the possibility of discussion presupposes some shared standards is a long way from saying that there is anything which is valuable for society as a whole. Since a society contains many different ways of life, it will also contain many different conceptions of good; the fact that these overlap, that they interact and modify each other, that some contain logical incoherences, does not mean that there is only one conception of good which is ultimately valid and that this is valid for society as a whole. For the phrase "society as a whole" does not characterize any one way of life. We talk sometimes, it is true, of the "western way of life," in order to draw a distinction between our type of society and certain others. But the western way of life, in this sense, contains many different ways of life in the sense in which I have been using the phrase in the preceding argument. Indeed, one of the most important ingredients of the western "way of life" is just the fact that in it different "ways of life" are recognized as valuable in themselves by people who are not themselves engaged in them.

At this point I should like to look more directly at the argument which lies behind the conception of university policy as needing to be directed towards enabling the universities to serve society. Industry, it is argued, needs technologists. Without an adequate supply of technologists British industry will lag behind foreign industry and the country as a whole will suffer. The universities can be so developed as to concentrate on the training of technologists; by training

[1]It is evident from this that the *content*, too, of this dialogue is highly relevant to the issue before us; as indeed is the whole course and nature of the conflict between Socrates and the Sophists. See John Anderson, "Socrates as an Educator," *Australasian Journal of Psychology and Philosophy*, IX (Sept. 1931), 172–84.

technologists they will be serving industry, and since society's greatest present need is for an industry which is as productive as possible, the universities will thus be serving society at the point where its need is greatest. Further, if this is not done, and the technologists are not produced for industry, there will just be a general economic collapse from which the universities would suffer as much as everybody else; so they really have no choice in the matter. These arguments may be supported by an appeal to the history of the universities; they have never, of course, been completely cut off from the rest of society and the various professions have always sought their recruits amongst graduates. So no radically new departure in policy is involved; the idea is simply to keep the universities in step with the times, as must happen if they are to survive or if, indeed, they are to be worthy of survival.

Now the most strikingly dramatic point in this argument is the suggestion of the danger of an all-engulfing general economic collapse. Let us grant that this danger is a real one; it will then, of course, be true that the universities will be as badly affected as anybody. But, first, I would remind those who are impressed by this argument that there is more than one way in which an institution may collapse or lose its distinctive character; besides being demolished from without it may also rot from within. As far as the universities are concerned, any departure from the fundamental concern with enquiry for its own sake would certainly constitute such a rot, since a concern with pure enquiry is what is above all distinctive about academic work. But, second, the dilemma is anyway a false one, since no one is denying the importance of having a sufficient number of trained technologists to participate in industrial production; the point is not even that the development of technology is not a legitimate concern of the universities. The point is rather whether the nature of the universities' concern with technology ought to be determined by any supposed "needs of society" (confusedly identified with the needs of industry). Quite apart from the question whether this is in the interests of the universities themselves, why should we suppose that it will necessarily be in the interests of technology and of industry?

If the Navy had laid down the sort of experts they wanted, these would still be expert builders of wooden sailing ships; if the Army had laid down the sort of experts they wanted these would still be horse-trainers and founders of bronze guns; if the chemical industry had laid down what sort of experts they wanted . . . there would be no chemical industry.[1]

This brings me to the argument from history; the plea that one of the main functions of the universities has always been to provide a supply of recruits to the professions in the shape of their graduates. Now the main stumbling block here is, of course, the word "function." It is true that certain of the professions have in fact always found the universities a valuable source of recruits. But this has not been because the universities have adapted their work to the needs of the professions concerned. The boot has been on the other foot. The professions have found the universities a valuable recruiting ground because they thought it good that their members should have a grounding in the academic outlook. So the argument from history works in my favour: in favour, that is, of the paramount necessity of maintaining the integrity of the academic outlook and of not subordinating it to the interests of any extraneous social movement.

What happens when these considerations are ignored is being horrifyingly exemplified by the position of Arts faculties in those institutions whose development is firmly in the grip of these forces which I am trying to oppose. The idea is spreading that one of the main "functions" of such faculties ought to be to "humanize" and "broaden" the outlook of science undergraduates by laying on special courses for them; this view is sometimes supported by the observation that it is, after all, the science graduates who are going to hold the positions of power in the society of the future, so if the universities are to play a dominant role in that society it is up to them to "do something" for such people. Now there may well be a strong case for special arts courses for science undergraduates, but if there is, the one I have outlined is not it. Any idea that one of the principal *raisons d'être* of an Arts faculty should be to provide such courses is death to any value such faculties may have, since it is surely self-evident that such value lies in their furtherance of the subjects with which they are charged and that their first and last responsibility must be *to* those subjects. *That* is the criterion according to which one ought to decide whether or not they are "pulling their weight" within the

[1]From "The Purpose of a University," a talk by Bertrand de Jouvenel on the B.B.C. Third Programme on August 9, 1956.

university. The conclusion is the same if the matter is looked at from the point of view of the best interests of students. What, ideally, a student gains from university study is an introduction to academic ways of working and thinking; he will obtain this best by contact with departments whose energies are devoted to the furtherance of such ways of working, not by having the departments concerned purvey to him something which they think to be in accordance with his supposed "needs." Of course, university teachers will be faced with the problem of how best to inculcate their peculiar ways of thinking to students at different stages of development. But that is different from the view that I am now criticizing, which involves too often courses of lectures which attempt a tabloid purveyance of neatly packaged results of other people's genuine thinking. This has got nothing to do with university education.

I have been emphasizing the importance of study and investigation as ends in themselves and insisting that the *raison d'être* of the universities is to further those ends for their own sakes and not as means to anything else. But I am not advocating that academic work should be treated as a closed mystery, or that every undergraduate should be regarded as carrying a professorial chair in his knapsack. To say that study is an attitude of mind and way of life with criteria and interests peculiar to itself is not to deny that someone who has been trained in that way of life may for that very reason be the more successful in quite different walks of life. To bring this out it is necessary to distinguish between the concept of the "life of an individual" and that of the "life of an institution." To speak of the life of an institution is, I have suggested, to speak of a specific tradition, a definite way of doing things, involving interests, methods and criteria peculiar to itself. But it would be a mistake to regard the life of an individual person in this circumscribed way. Just as a society contains many different ways of life, so does an individual participate in many different ways of life. And the ways in which the various kinds of activity in which a person participates influence each other (and therefore him) in the course of his life may be compared to the ways in which different forms of activity may influence each other within a whole society. Only if academic institutions maintain the integrity of their own specific ways of working will academic training continue to be of value to someone who proposes to devote most of his life to the service of some other institution.

Finally, I should like to make some general remarks about the hierarchy of values presupposed by someone who wishes to determine the direction of policies (for the universities and other institutions) by reference to the supposed "needs of society." I have remarked that this frequently involves deriving the needs of society from the needs of industry. This derivation is usually made by way of the consumptive concept of "welfare"; it involves thinking industry important because of the satisfaction people get out of consuming its products—cars, television sets, washing machines, etc. Now consumption, if it is regarded as an end in itself, rather than as facilitating productive activities, represents a sort of lowest common denominator in a society. Although people's consumptive tastes do differ to some extent, they do so far less than do the productive activities in which they engage; and where consumptive tastes do differ this is most often to be explained in terms of differences in their possessors' mode of (productive) life. A move towards emphasis on consumption, towards thinking productive activities worthwhile only from the point of view of what they enable people to consume, and away from regarding consumption as valuable only insofar as it is important for some productive activity, is a move towards the ironing out of free independent activity. This involves an increase in the power of the state at the expense of the autonomy of independent productive movements, which have always been recognized by the advocates of absolute state power as a threat to their ideal. Hobbes was very hostile to the universities, regarding them as responsible for dispensing a "subtle liquor against the civil authority," and advocating that their teaching should be brought under the supervision of the political sovereign. The implications of this are worth pondering in relation to recent discussions about the duties of university workers towards state security agencies. Industry itself has naturally been subject to the same dialectic: trades unions have concentrated on the *welfare* of their members, which they have tried to further very largely by means of state legislation. In so doing they have raised the workers' material standards of living considerably; but the workers are, if anything, even farther away than they once were from any prospect of real control over the conditions of their work, which has become concentrated in state-controlled boards. There are disturbing analogies here for anybody contemplating the present state of the universities—their dependence on the government for finance and their acquiescence in developments for non-academic purposes.

Anyone who asks "why society should pay" for other people to cultivate the life of enquiry if that does not contribute to material well-being is clearly thinking of a society of consumers. He is ignoring the importance of productive activities, for in terms of these there is no homogeneous entity called "society," only a multitude of competing and interacting ways of life. Any of these can be valuable if pursued for its own sake; but if one thinks of them all in terms of some external criterion of value—that of consumption or "welfare"— one takes away what is really valuable in any of them.

Perhaps some will agree with the principle of my argument, but will find it unrealistic as the basis for any practical attitude. They will argue that since the universities *are* now dependent on industry and the state for funds, they can only develop by acquiescing in the external demands made upon them. The appropriate reply to this has been made very forcefully by Professor John Anderson, of Sydney:

> The University can demand State support on the ground that it does pre-pare for the professions and that it alone, precisely because of its disinterested approach to the questions involved, can do so efficiently. It follows, however, that it cannot accept State control of the administration of funds, or any State interference in its policy. The forces which go by the name of "the State" do not understand the conditions necessary for the maintenance of academic standards, and have a definitely commercialist bias. . . . Only an aggressive policy can enable the University to maintain its standards in these times; and such a policy, with the greater academic freedom it would entail, would stimulate the support of graduates instead of allowing them to drift easily into the commercialist camp.[1]

The universities possess a great deal of independent authority; they stand for a way of life generally thought valuable. The preservation of that way of life is of more long-term importance than is any immediate economic crisis, any immediate expansion. If the universities compromise and go under in the utilitarian flood, they will lose their authority and commit suicide much more effectively than they will by refusing immediate opportunities to expand in the wrong directions and for the wrong reasons.

[1]"University Reform," *Australasian Journal of Psychology and Philosophy*, XIII (Sept. 1935), 220–1.

The Refining Fire :
The Meaning and Use of Poetry

By A. J. M. SMITH

IN APPROACHING the problem of what a poem is, what it means, or what it communicates, I would ask you to put out of your minds any preconceived opinions about the nature, purposes, or methods of poetry. Put aside, if you can, such arbitrary generalizations about the nature of poetry as that it is, or ought to be, emotional; that it must be "elevated"; it must be "beautiful"; it must deal with "poetic" subjects. Where these notions are not too hopelessly vague, they have validity, but their main tendency is to limit and dilute our appreciation and cloud our understanding. The subject matter of poetry is much wider in scope, more immediate and less selective, much less respectable and much more intense than most of us realize.

Let us think of a poem rather than of poetry; and let us attempt a working definition. It might go something like this. A poem is a highly organized, complex, and unified re-creation of experience in which the maximum use of meaning and suggestion in the sounds of words has been achieved with the minimum essential outlay of words. A poem is not the description of an experience, it is itself an experience, and it awakens in the mind of the alert and receptive reader a new experience analogous to the one in the mind of the poet ultimately responsible for the creation of the poem. The more sensitive the reader and the better instructed he is the closer will his experience be to that of the poet. It is almost as difficult, and quite as important, to be a good reader as to be a good poet.

Yet it is not, I would like to maintain, the nature of it, or the moral respectability of the emotions that produced it or rose out of, or even the immediate, practical, sentimental consequences that appear to flow from it, that make a poem good rather than bad or valuable rather than dangerous. Too often a poem is thought to achieve morality and usefulness and *does* achieve popularity through

Reprinted from *Queen's Quarterly*, LXI (Autumn, 1954), 353–64.

an unconsciously hypocritical failure to pierce uncompromisingly through to the heart of an experience which would have become too bitter and too painful had the poet dared to descend more deeply into it. The great poets are those who have dared to descend more deeply into the heart of reality, and some of them have found the way there through the emotions of hate, fear, lust, anger, and despair. The names of Raleigh, Donne, Pope, Swift, Hardy, and the author of *King Lear* are not the least honoured among poets.

At this point we must ask: If the worth of a poem is not to be found in the nature of the re-created experience or in the morality or cheerfulness of its resolution, where is it to be found? Upon what does it depend?

The answer is that the value of a poem lies in the intensity with which an experience has been encountered, and the accuracy with which its consequences, good or evil, delightful or painful, have been recognized and accepted. It is the integrity, the clarity, and the completeness with which an experience is met, whether it is trivial, harsh, ugly, magnificent, or delightful, that counts in the evaluation not only of a poem's goodness but also of its usefulness. The nature of the experience, as such, has nothing to do with the genuineness or the goodness of the poem, and no preconceived opinion can postulate the special conditions under which the right intensity of pressure will be generated.

It follows that there are no "poetic" subjects. Any subject, no matter how unpromising, can be made the source of poetry when shaped by the poetic imagination. Accuracy of perception and concentrated clarity of expression—what might, in its finest manifestation, be called "nakedness of vision"—can make the humblest and even the vilest material a source of poetry, so that a poem is not only a re-creation of experience but also a transfiguration of experience, or, in Joycean terms, an epiphany.

Let me cite a particular example to demonstrate *what is done* in a poem and also, in part, *how* it is done. Here is a poem of eight lines by the contemporary American poet William Carlos Williams in which with remarkable concentration we are given a new and surprising vision of something we may often have looked at but have never actually seen with the eye of the imagination until the poet showed it to us. It is called "Flowers by the Sea."

When over the flowery sharp pasture's
edge, unseen, the salt ocean

lifts its form—chickory and daisies
tied, released, seem hardly flowers alone

but color and the movement—or the shape
perhaps—of restlessness, whereas

the sea is circled and sways
peacefully upon its plantlike stem

Brief and clear as it is, this little poem states, or rather illustrates, a paradox—the paradox that the sea and the pasture each suggests the other's basic nature rather than its own. But the curious thing is that the unexpected reversal of images which makes the point of the poem emerges suddenly, only after we have absorbed the whole dazzling picture of the sunny windswept seaside field and felt the tousled salt-laden atmosphere of the summer day. The first unexpected identification is that of the restless amalgam of colour and movement in the flowers and grasses—"the shape, perhaps, of restlessness"—with the ebb and flow ("tied, released") of the waves; and, parallel to it, but much richer and grander, is the sudden awareness of the vast blue round of the ocean itself, swaying like an enormous flower. There has indeed been a sea-change into something rich and strange, and, most daringly, the magic has been performed in the realm of the familiar, not in that of the exotic.

"Flowers by the Sea" expresses an experience, which culminates for both poet and reader in the intuitive flash at the close, when it is perceived not that the flowers and the sea are like one another in some respects but that the flowers *are* a sea and the sea *is* a flower. The imagination leaves out all but the common qualities shared by the flowers and the waves, all but colour and movement, that is—all but the blue circular shape and the swaying motion. Here intense concentration upon what the senses and the imagination have isolated leads to a form of truth that is more limited but more precious than the truth of science or fact, for it is a truth perceived simultaneously by the heart, the imagination, and the mind. In this poem sense impressions received from the fluid, elusively beautiful object of attention seem all important. And they *are* all important, but not— even in a poem so self-contained and self-justifying as this one—for themselves alone, or as the generating source of emotion. What gives the poem its point and its tang is the paradoxical reversal of ordinary experience, when in a flash the flowers are seen as a sea and the sea as a flower—and this is an *intellectual* act. Although what touches the emotions here is first the evocation of all the delight that gathers round the sunny windswept landscape of flowers by the dancing sea, it is finally the exhilaration that accompanies the perception of a paradox. Not in metaphysical poetry only does intellectual action, whether slowly or swiftly brought to a consummation, resolve itself in emotion when it comes to its successful and dramatic conclusion.

2

These considerations have carried us far away from the popular conception of poetry as something flowery, vague, and conventional in a "nice" and undisturbing way. If that widespread conception were at all true, poetry would of course be much simpler than it is— and much less interesting. It would be like any other gesture or experience that lacked passion, originality, or intelligent direction. Not such easy things as vagueness and "niceness" but difficult things —precision and intensity—are the marks of the genuine in poetry.

It is true, however, that these marks of the genuine are to be found in two sharply contrasted types of poetry: the positive, traditional poetry which we easily recognize as universal and optimistic; and the negative, unorthodox poetry that tells unpleasant truths. Both kinds are true and valuable in their separate ways, and indeed there are many instances of a poet's writing in both moods at different times, and occasionally in the same work. Let us briefly consider each in turn.

Poetry, certainly, most often expresses ideas and emotions felt generally by all mankind to be true in the long run to the common experience of humanity. Such poetry is simple, affirmative, conservative, "acceptable," and genuinely popular. It does not make its appeal by its originality or its unexpectedness, or even by its profundity, but by its convincing rightness, by the *felt* truth with which it confirms people in what they have come to feel and believe without ever having been able to put it into memorable words. This is the idea of Pope's classical conception of poetry as "What oft was thought but ne'er so well expressed" and of Keats's well-known statement: "I think poetry should surprise by a fine excess, and not by singularity. It should strike the reader as a wording of his own highest thoughts, and appear almost a remembrance."

Poems and images fitting these descriptions are immediately satisfying; they are accepted at once and never forgotten. Lines whose impressiveness are of this order are the easiest to call to mind:

> She walks in beauty like the night
> (Byron)

> I wandered lonely as a cloud
> (Wordsworth)

> The day is done and the darkness
> Falls from the wings of night
> As a feather is wafted downward
> From an eagle in his flight.
> (Longfellow)

> The uncertain glory of an April day
> (Shakespeare)

The rightness and what one might perhaps call the unviolent nostalgia of these images are among the chief factors contributing to their effectiveness. Good popular poetry derives its strength from the fact that it soothes and reassures rather than challenges and surprises us. The attitude toward experience and the evaluation of it are in harmony with the most commonly accepted and generally valid views of mankind.

But the poet has always had another function to perform. His eye is sharper than that of the ordinary person, and like the prophet—or, as Louis MacNeice has said, like the informer—he has always made it part of his business to see the "other side" of things and to present feelings and attitudes that shock or undermine everything that has been too complacently accepted. Images and poems in this mode are not necessarily more difficult to understand than those in the mode of "acceptance." But it is perhaps more difficult for the poet of the unusual and the unaccepted to overcome the prejudices of his readers and to force a recognition of what had hitherto been hidden or repressed.

This distinction between the two types of poetry—that which confirms and reassures and that which shocks or disturbs—extends to the style itself, especially to the handling of images and figurative language. If we place beside the beautiful lines just quoted parallel images of this second kind, we discover that in the latter group the distance between the two arms of the comparison (between, for instance, the brightness of God and the depth of darkness in the first quotation below) is much greater; the things compared in a simile or identified in a metaphor are not nearly so easily seen to be alike. And the effect is not to confirm us in what we already feel but to startle us awake so that we become aware of something not experienced before:

> There is in God (some say)
> A deep but dazzling darkness.
> (Henry Vaughan)

> I should have been a pair of ragged claws
> Scuttling across the floors of silent seas.
> (Eliot)

> The fine fine wind that takes its course through
> the chaos of the world
> Like an exquisite chisel, a wedgeblade inserted. . . .
> (D. H. Lawrence)

> A serpent swam a vertex to the sun
> On unpaced beaches leaned its
> tongue and drummed.
> What fountains did I hear? What icy speeches?
> (Hart Crane)

> April is the cruelest month. . . .
> (Eliot)

Lines like these, and the poems they are taken from, reveal the poet in his most valuable role—as the uncoverer of the hidden secrets of the human consciousness and as the conscience of society.

I shall develop this point in a moment, but first I wish to mitigate its seeming harshness. No matter how subversive of human self-esteem, how disillusioned or bitter a poet's philosophical outlook may be, it is always delight and love that are at the heart of his writing, idealizing the world of sensation and making it human. This delight and love are first and foremost a passion of the eye, a sort of visual thirst that drinks eagerly whatever it lights upon: "Eye, gazelle, delicate wanderer, drinker of horizon's fluid line"—as Stephen Spender has expressed it; and accuracy and vividness are never sacrificed to ornament or faked emotion—at least in genuine poetry they are not. Accuracy, which is a kind of faithfulness and sincerity, is one of the special marks of high excellence. Consider Browning's

> The wild tulip at end of its tube blows out its great red bell
> Like a thin clear bubble of blood

or Whitman's

> Earth of the vitreous pour of the full moon just tinged
>   with blue!
> Earth of shine and dark mottling the tide of the river!

or Herrick's synthesis of several of the sense impressions:

> Whenas in silks my *Julia* goes,
> Then, then, methinks, how sweetly flowes
> The liquefaction of her clothes.
>
> Next, when I cast mine eyes and see
> That brave Vibration each way free;
> O how that glittering taketh me!

or Marianne Moore's curiously comparable sound-picture, as she describes a ship's boat moving over the ocean:

> —the blades of the oars
> moving together like the feet of water-spiders . . . .
> The wrinkles progress upon themselves in a phalanx—beautiful
>   under networks of foam
> and fade breathlessly while the sea rustles in and out of the
>   seaweed. . . .

Each of these passages illustrates in its own way how the poet looks at, and listens to, the world around him, transmuting it with the glow of his own delight into that "golden" realm which Sir Philip Sidney declared to be beyond nature.

3

What, it is time to ask, is the special, unique, and characteristic use of the perceptiveness and accuracy with which a poet responds to experience?—*use*, I mean, to the reader? and to society?

Its first and most fundamental use—first and most fundamental because all other possible uses must come through or grow out of this one—is the training, developing, exercising, and strengthening of the sensibilities themselves, so that our perceptions of physical things are made at once sharper, subtler, more penetrating and also stronger and more intense. And, in turn, in the well-tempered personality, the training of poetry and art helps to develop a corresponding purification and strengthening of the emotional and intellectual faculties.

This is why the neglect or perversion of criticism in our schools and colleges, and indeed in our culture generally, is so serious a matter. We have forgotten, or perhaps have not yet fully realized, that the reading of imaginative literature is itself an art—both a fine art and a useful art, an art that involves perception, apprehension, and evaluation—and that to neglect it or merely to pay it lip-service or to substitute vague appreciation for the hard work and discipline that is involved in the technique of accurate reading: to do any of these things is to corrupt the spiritual life of the community. Today we have special problems. As the dramatic critic, Eric Bentley, wrote recently: "We have destroyed the old aristocratic culture, which, for all its faults had a place for the arts, and have created a culture of commodities, which to be sure has a place for everything —upon one condition: that everything become a commodity. Thus there is one sort of literature that flourishes today as never before: commodity literature as promoted by the book clubs and publishers' salesmen."[1]

This same point of view has been behind the critical activity of Mr. F. R. Leavis and his group of scholars and critics at Cambridge. In the first issue of their magazine *Scrutiny* in 1932, Mr. Leavis spoke for those who see a connection between the plight of the arts in the modern world and the present drift of civilization. The arts, he affirmed, are more than a luxury product. He described them in Arnoldian terms as "the storehouse of recorded values," and went on to say in a sentence whose validity I have assumed throughout this essay, that "there is a necessary relationship between the quality of an individual's response to art and his general fitness for humane existence."[2] Another of the Cambridge school of scholar-critics, Mr. L. C. Knights, has stressed the value for the humanities of the discipline involved in the perceptive study of literature. "The reading of literature, insofar as it is anything more than a pastime," declares Mr. Knights, "involves the continuous development of the power of intelligent discrimination. Literature, moreover, is simply the exact expression of realized values. It is part of the artist's function to give precise meaning to ideas and sentiments that are only obscurely perceived by his contemporaries."[3]

[1]E. R. Bentley, ed., *The Importance of Scrutiny* (New York: G. W. Stewart, 1948), xviii.

[2]*Ibid.*, 3.

[3]*Explorations* (London: Chatto and Windus, 1946), 193.

This conception of the poet's function is in harmony with what I was saying earlier about the poet and artist as prophet, medicineman, and informer. I pick up the word "informer" from Louis MacNeice, who speaks of the poet as a blend of the informer and the entertainer. He means "informer" in the "bad" sense of the word. The poet is one who *tells on us.* He is our secret conscience. He reveals hidden and uncomfortable truths. He lets light and air into dark, closed places. He pricks the wounds of the unconscious and prevents them from festering. He exposes suppressed evil, and can make us whole again.

The same thought is expressed as the climactic idea in R. G. Collingwood's great work, *The Principles of Art.* After an acute analysis of one of the greatest and most representative of modern masterpieces, T. S. Eliot's *The Waste Land,* Collingwood brings his study of art to a conclusion with the following pertinent summary:

> To readers who want not amusement or magic, but poetry, and who want to know what poetry can be if it is to be neither of these things, *The Waste Land* supplies an answer. And by reflecting on it we can perhaps detect one more characteristic which art must have, if it is to forgo both entertainment-value and magical value, and draw a subject matter from its audience themselves. It must be prophetic. The artist must prophesy not in the sense that he foretells things to come, but in the sense that he tells his audience, at risk of their displeasure, the secrets of their own hearts. His business as an artist is to speak out, to make a clean breast. But what he has to utter is not, as the individualistic theory of art would have us think, his own secrets. As spokesman of his community, the secrets he must utter are theirs. The reason why they need him is that no community altogether knows its own heart; and by failing in this knowledge a community deceives itself on the one subject concerning which ignorance means death. For the evils which come from that ignorance the poet as prophet suggests no remedy, because he has already given one. The remedy is the poem itself. Art is the community's medicine for the worst disease of mind, the corruption of consciousness.[1]

Poetry, we may add, is the prime and essential art in the performance of this function, for the poet makes us re-examine our perceptions and teaches us to keep our words, and therefore our ideas, clean and precise.

The perceptive reading of poetry, then—an activity which involves the discipline of criticism but which always must return to pleasure and delight—is seen as a useful action. It has a practical value, and it involves an interplay not only between the poet as an individual and the individual reader but between both and the community.

[1] *The Principles of Art* (Oxford: Clarendon Press, 1933), 335-6.

Shelley was aware of this when he wrote in his *Defence of Poetry*:

> A man to be greatly good, must imagine intensely and comprehensively; he must put himself in the place of another and of many others; the pains and pleasures of his species must become his own. . . . Whatever strengthens and purifies the affections, enlarges the imagination, and adds spirit to sense, is useful.

Never more useful—do I need to add?—than here and now, in the present crisis of world affairs, when, as the Anglo-American poet, W. H. Auden, has put it, "We must love one another or die."

4

Professor Collingwood, who was a philosopher and a historian, boldly extended the realm of the classic to include the masterpieces of our own time. This is only proper. To be afraid to do so is to impugn the validity of your critical principles and indeed of your scholarship. And it is to be something considerably less than completely useful. For it is also the task of scholarship and criticism to discover, explore, and evaluate the modern work that lifts itself above the ordinary and, pushing back into the past and forward into the future, proclaims itself a classic.

Are there none such? Can we not discern them? Can we not apply the same standards of measurement that time and the scholar-critics have applied to the classics of the past (clarity, wholeness, integrity, depth, intensity, universality) and separate the works of permanent excellence from the slick, the exciting, the charming, or the meretricious? At least we must try. And so, to conclude, I shall attempt to sum up briefly what we may learn about the terrible age we live in from the testimony of the great modern classics of the creative imagination.

A consideration of these reveals a common rejection of objective realism as a literary method and of social amelioration as an end. The causes of the decay of civilization as expressed in the poetry of Eliot and the fiction of Proust and Joyce are seen to be metaphysical and religious—the result of ways of feeling and habits of mind produced by the mechanization of the surface of life and the secularization of thought. In reaction to this, the modern masters have sought the recovery of myth and in some cases of dogma: in Yeats an esoteric and eclectic magical dogma, in Eliot a catholic and Christian one. As Northrop Frye has written:

The age that produced the hell of Rimbaud and the angels of Rilke, Kafka's castle and James's ivory tower, the spirals of Yeats and the hermaphrodites of Proust, the intricate dying-god symbolism attached to Christ in Eliot and the exhaustive treatment of Old Testament myths in Mann's study of Joseph, is once again a great mythopoeic age.[1]

The work of the re-establishment of order has begun by the analysis of a dying chaos in *Ulysses* and *Remembrance of Things Past* and by the exploration of the moral confusion of our time in Gide and James and Kafka. All these masters of the creative imagination, these poets whether they write in prose or verse, are united in a common task, and they are in agreement with their nineteenth-century forerunners, Dostoievsky, Baudelaire, and Rimbaud, that the heart of the matter lies in the problem of guilt and suffering. The wisdom to be derived in the final analysis from modern imaginative literature is that responsibility must be accepted once more as a spiritual reality before the individual can be restored to grace or society to civilization. Although the picture that emerges from the great prophetic literature of our time is one of isolation, horror, and suffering, the suffering has been wilfully and consciously entered into by the creative imagination. "In the destructive element immerse: that is the way."

But the modern world is not Hell; the suffering is not eternal nor infinite nor hopeless. It is rather the refining fire into which Arnaut Daniel in the *Purgatorio* dived back, because, as he said to Virgil, "I see with joy the day for which I hope before me."

[1] *Fearful Symmetry: A Study of William Blake* (Princeton: Princeton University Press, 1947), 223.

Recent Shakespearean Criticism

By R. S. KNOX

THE FIRST HALF of the twentieth century, and more especially the last thirty years, with which this survey is mainly concerned, has seen an unprecedented activity in the study and criticism of Shakespeare's drama. Older views have been re-assessed, new critical directions have been vigorously explored, and a more informed and searching scholarship has been brought to bear on the varied problems of the plays. One obvious reason for this heightened activity is not far to seek: the ever growing army of academic scholars, among them some of our most distinguished critics, who have added valuably to our knowledge not only through the medium of scholarly monographs but as well in the hundreds of articles contributed annually to the learned journals. Indeed this growth in academic research is perhaps the most striking aspect of Shakespearean and other studies in our time. If the hope of unbaring the heart of Shakespeare's mystery depends on the number of doctors operating and the variety of their instruments, then the prospect is bright. The periodical articles, however, often the bases for more extensive studies, must for present purposes be passed over.

In the field of scholarship, if for convenience that may be distinguished from criticism, first place must be given to the continuation of the work on the play texts, on the problems of transmission, authenticity, revision, and chronology. Early in the century a new lead had been given by a brilliant band of scholars, A. W. Pollard, E. K. Chambers, R. B. McKerrow, W. W. Greg, and J. Dover Wilson; and in 1930 their views were summarized and discussed by Chambers in the two volumes of his *William Shakespeare*. Among more recent contributions in this field two might be singled out: P. Alexander's convincing proof that *The Contention* and *The True Tragedy* are bad quartos of the second and third parts of *Henry VI*, and G. I. Duthie's almost convincing solution of the problem of the *Hamlet* first quarto. Most of these textual scholars, it may be said, have frowned upon J. M. Robertson's bold contention that many of the plays in the canon cannot be considered as wholly Shakespeare's work, although Dover Wilson still occasionally expresses his doubts and T. S. Eliot in his essay on *Hamlet*[1] seems to have listened to Robertson.

In the early decades of the century the dominating critic was certainly A. C. Bradley. His profound and imaginative analyses of the plays in *Shakespearean Tragedy* (1904) can be regarded as the grand climax of romantic criticism. For a whole generation his book on the tragedies was, as it were, the Shakespeare student's bible, and indeed it still remains a classic of criticism. The degree of his influence and a hint of the subsequent partial reaction are caught in the well-known jingle:

> I dreamt that William Shakespeare's ghost
> Tried for a Civil Service post.
> The examination for that year
> Was on *Hamlet* and *King Lear*.
> William, I fear, did very badly,
> You see, he had not read his Bradley.

E. E. Stoll was Bradley's most clamorous opponent. In book after book he sought to refute what he considered the Bradley fallacy, the tendency to impose a real life psychology on the characters, ignoring the fact that poetic drama transmutes life for its own deeper purposes by art and artifice.[2] Situation not character, Stoll insisted, is the core of drama. There is no need to labour the opposition. Most of us have probably come to some compromise position. We give grateful homage to Bradley even if we admit that he and more markedly some of his followers have been excessively preoccupied with characterization. We allow that Stoll brings a healthy corrective, although he too runs to excesses on the other side. But the controversy is still alive. H. B. Charlton in his book, *Shakespearean Tragedy*, proclaims himself a staunch Bradleyite, and J. I. M. Stewart in *Character and Motive in Shakespeare* would bring psychoanalysis to counter the charge of psychological inconsistencies in the characters. T. S. Eliot has a sensible compromise comment. While he holds that it is wrong to dwell on character to the neglect of other aspects of the play (which, of course, Bradley never does), yet he admits that to abstract a figure is "a perfectly legitimate form of criticism though liable to abuses; at its best it can add very much to our enjoyment of the moments of the characters' life which are given in the scene, if we feel this richness of reality in them."[3]

Many of the recent critics have taken what may be vaguely called the historical approach to the plays. This, of course, is no

twentieth-century novelty, but it has been proclaimed more than
ever before as the direction from which the plays can be most profitably viewed. We must, it is increasingly claimed, see Shakespeare in
his original environment, his art in terms of Elizabethan thought
and culture and in the setting of the drama and theatre of his time.
Dover Wilson has been one of the foremost in demanding the
Elizabethan Shakespeare. By his knowledge of Elizabethan ghost
lore and methods of staging, he has sought to correct our notions of
what is happening in *Hamlet*. Miss Lily Campbell in her *Shakespeare's Histories* insists not only that we must read the English
history plays as mirrors of Elizabethan policy, as in a sense we surely
can, but also that we must associate their figures with definite persons
of Shakespeare's age, which, judging by her examples, is more than
doubtful. Nor is she alone in assuring us of these identifications.
Dover Wilson sees Essex in several of the plays; Middleton Murry
chooses Southampton. E. M. W. Tillyard more cautiously interprets
the histories in terms of Elizabethan political ideas; and he gives in
his *Elizabethan World Picture* the assumptions about the universe
which the age accepted. The dominant conception, it is pointed out,
is of an ordered universe with each created thing in its appointed
place; and Shakespeare's concern in his plays with order and the
calamities issuing from disorder is duly demonstrated. A. Harbage,
who likes to poke fun at the Elizabethan frame of reference, has his
cool and slightly malicious comment:

The three speeches in Shakespeare most commonly quoted in our chaotic
times as expressing the poet's personal convictions are those on order and
degree by the Archbishop of Canterbury in *Henry V*, by Ulysses in *Troilus
and Cressida*, and by Menenius in *Coriolanus*. One is inclined to agree that
Shakespeare, since few people favour chaos, believed in the main import of
these speeches. We may set this down to coincidence. That he was pausing
at these three moments to inculcate principles is another matter. Perhaps one
can be too fastidious in requiring disinterestedness in one's philosophers, but
it cannot be ignored that each of the three speeches is delivered by an
unscrupulous politician meeting an immediate problem—advocating a practical
program of somewhat debatable merit.[4]

In many of these historical studies the stress is on the mediaeval
element in Elizabethan thought. It is the theme of W. Farnham's
book, *The Medieval Heritage of Elizabethan Tragedy*, and of
Shakespeare and the Nature of Man, where T. Spencer interestingly
if at times forcibly reads the plays in terms of the Renaissance
conflict. A corrective to those who too violently press the history

plays into an Elizabethan setting is J. Palmer's *Political Characters of Shakespeare*. He would admit, of course, that Shakespeare accepted the ideology of his time, but he holds:

The astonishing veracity of Shakespeare's political characters is due to the small interest which he took in politics as compared with the great interest he took in human nature. His main concern was not so much in the policies as with the men who made them.[5]

Moreover he points out that, when the plays are compared with the known sources, the dramatist's additions elaborate and vivify more often the personal than the political situations.

Again, there is the insistence that to understand the plays we must be aware of the dramatic and theatrical conventions which were accepted in Shakespeare's time. Early in the century L. Schücking in his *Character Problems in Shakespeare's Plays* had claimed to show the survival of primitive techniques. Stoll's main thesis had been that, in ignoring the Elizabethan dramatic traditions and conventions, we were mis-reading Shakespeare's art. Recently, this question has been re-examined, more calmly by Miss Bradbrook in her *Themes and Conventions of Elizabethan Tragedy*, and more daringly by S. L. Bethell in his *Shakespeare and the Popular Dramatic Tradition* where he would show in the plays a deliberate blend of conventionalism and naturalism and argues for the "multi-consciousness" of the Elizabethan audience, its ability to respond in several ways at once.

It was in the early thirties that a quite fresh approach to the plays first became clearly evident. The shift showed itself in the new or at least intensified interest in the texture of the language of the plays and in their imagery. W. Empson published his *Seven Types of Ambiguity*, revealing the diverse import of the word. *Aspects of Elizabethan Imagery* by Miss Holmes appeared in 1929 and about the same time the first of Miss Spurgeon's studies. In 1934 came Miss Spurgeon's full investigation, *Shakespeare's Imagery and What It Tells Us*. We may discount her claim to throw light on the poet's personality from the evidence of the images he used, but her cataloguing of the dominant and recurring imagery, with coloured charts to help, has since evoked many subtler studies, such as that on the development and dramatic use of the imagery by the German critic, W. Clemen. It has been often said that each age looks in the art of the past for what especially interests itself, and there is no doubt that the present concern with imagery and symbol as perhaps the basic element in the play's structure and meaning is in accord with the practice of contemporary poetry, and indeed of the other arts. But, as we look back, we see that the most influential publication of the early thirties was G. Wilson Knight's book, *The Wheel of Fire*. We may disagree with some of his contentions here, his reading of *Hamlet* for example, but we are forced to admit that he more than anyone else has been followed in later Shakespearean criticism. Wilson Knight calls himself not a critic but an interpreter. He draws the distinction most precisely in the Preface to *The Wheel of Fire*, and there puts forward his views on the nature of Shakespeare's art. Criticism, he contends, is a judgment of the play's vision; interpretation is a reconstruction of the vision, translating it into discursive reasoning. Interpretation asserts the validity of the poetic unit; if the play is understood in its totality, any supposed faults vanish. A Shakespearean tragedy is set spatially as well as temporally in the mind; there is a set of correspondences which relate to each other independently of the time-sequence which is the story. The play must be seen as a visionary whole, close-knit in personification, atmospheric suggestion, and direct poetic symbolism. Interpretation, he insists, is not concerned with the dramatist's intentions or his sources or with characters as they are morally regarded. An interpretation must be metaphysical rather than ethical. And Wilson Knight gives his opinion of both the older criticism and its supposed corrective:

The older critics drove psychological analysis to unnecessary lengths; the new school of realistic "criticism," in finding faults and explaining them with regard to Shakespeare's purely practical or financial "intentions," are thus in reality following the wrong vision of their predecessors; . . . neither touches the heart of the Shakespearean play.[6]

Even at the cost of repetition it is worthwhile considering some of the implications of these views. For the purpose of interpretation we need not, it seems, look beyond the play itself; the text or the performance is all we require, although the play in hand should be related to the rest of the dramatist's work. The quest for the Elizabethan Shakespeare, the concern with influences, dramatic traditions, etc., all valid interests in themselves, have little or no bearing on our interpretation. The question of possible non-Shakespearean work or of revision is rightly regarded as of no importance if Shakespeare is assumed to be the last handler of the play. As to Shakespeare's intentions, it may certainly be asked how we are to know them except from the plays themselves. Shakespeare was presumably aware of what he intended to do, but he has left no guiding comments as some of his fellow dramatists have done. Nor can we deny that art may have significances beyond the consciousness of the artist. On the other hand, the artist can certainly be surprised, as T. S. Eliot confesses with regard to his poetry, at what his interpreters may find. A well-known Canadian painter has a pertinent comment. He had painted a picture into which he had brought a telegraph pole with its cross-beam and a repairman leaning over the beam. It was a fairly commonplace, realistic composition. The painter tells how he was staggered when an interpreter admiringly approached him: "Ah, I see what you mean, a beautiful symbol of the crucifixion of the worker." Can we forbid this interpreter his response?

A work of art, a poetic drama, it may be argued, is what we each make of it. An interesting defence of that view is given by Lascelles Abercrombie, but he has one important qualification:

When I say a play exists in what it means to any one who will receive it, the implication is plain, that everything is excluded from that existence which is not given by the author's technique. The existence of a work of art is completed by the recipient's attention to what the author says to him; whatever may come in through inattention to that does not belong to the art at all.[7]

And T. S. Eliot, referring to some readings of Shakespeare's plays, gives a salutary reminder that "a mystical treatise is at best a poor substitute for the original experience of the author."[8] The acceptance by others of an interpretation will obviously depend on the quality of the interpreter. We are not all equally gifted for this work. Wilson Knight is one of the few to whom we can profitably listen, as in his essays on *King Lear* and on "The Othello Music," which are already classics of Shakespearean criticism—or rather interpretation.

The reading of the plays "spatially" and in terms of their symbols and imagery is at present almost the dominant practice. One recent example might be cited, R. B. Heilman's *This Great Stage: Image and Structure in* King Lear. Heilman acknowledges his debt to Wilson Knight, and his method falls in with that of the American "new" critics, who hold that a poem or play should be examined only according to its own inner organization. In *King Lear*, he would show, there are key words, recurrent comments on certain themes, which, in relation to the images and to the dramatic facts, build up a series of ideas embodying the total statement of the play. Each pattern becomes a symbol "for the problems which arise in connection with the point of view from which man judges the meaning of experience."[9] There are the patterns of sight, clothes, nature, and madness, the last being the core of the play. In the mad scenes the other patterns are bound together, and the key phrase is Edgar's "reason in madness." There we have expressed Shakespeare's profoundest comment on human experience, and Heilman tells us what it is:

King Lear dramatises fundamentally the paradox that wisdom and insight may be found in the outcast and deranged, and that the powerful and brilliant may be, by both moral and pragmatic standards, insane; it amplifies this dramatic theme by the contributory paradoxes that those best equipped with eyesight in the world may be blind to spiritual truths, that those who in strength and ruthlessness are like animals may have destroying weaknesses, and that the gorgeously arrayed may lose the most important of all defences.[10]

Heilman's analysis in terms of patterns, although carried to undue extremes, does in the main correspond to the normal imaginative response to the play and often deepens our understanding of it. On the other hand, his summing up of the meaning of King Lear turns the play into a rather commonplace sermon.

Another approach to Shakespeare's drama in vogue at present issues from the growing interest in anthropology. This is exemplified in Gilbert Murray's book, Hamlet and Orestes, and more comprehensively in Miss Bodkin's Archetypal Patterns in Poetry. Miss Bodkin defines her purpose as an attempt to identify in tragic poetry "themes having a particular form or pattern which persists amid variation from age to age and which corresponds to a pattern or configuration of emotional tendencies in the minds of those who are stirred by the theme."[11] This digging down to the mysterious springs of art creation, this searching in Shakespeare's drama for primordial themes, is in itself very interesting, even if it may not throw much light on the dramatist's art or on the merit of the play. Shakespeare, of course, was probably not aware of this aspect of the stories he chose, unlike those twentieth-century poets who consciously use the archetypal symbols. Miss Bodkin extracts from the tragedies her examples: the Rebirth, the theme of Heaven and Hell, the Father figure, the tragic hero's death as the atoning sacrifice. Many varieties of these archetypes have since been read into other plays, more especially into the final group of Romances.

The prevalent concern in the most recent criticism, as this survey has tried to show, has been with the imagery and symbolism of the plays, with the plays, one might almost say, as dramatic poems; and few would deny the further reaches of Shakespeare's art which have thus been opened. But great art such as Shakespeare's has many related aspects. In our concern with the poetry we may have tended to lose sight of the drama as that presents the characters and actions of men. That danger the theatre itself can best avert; and for a full appreciation of the play, criticism must always take second place to what is gained by the vivid life of the stage. Fortunately, the period under review has been as distinguished in its Shakespearean productions as in its criticism. Indeed, one of the best of the period's critics, H. Granville-Barker, was both producer and actor, and in his *Prefaces to Shakespeare's Plays* he has brilliantly demonstrated his twofold gift of revealing the subtleties of the dramatist's art, especially in character creation, and of showing how best the plays can be fitted to the theatre. He and William Poel, his teacher, were the modern pioneers in giving us the plays practically as they were written, with the minimum of cuts and with no unwarranted elaborations. Their lead has since been worthily followed, and today, in the best productions of London's Old Vic or Canada's Stratford, we have Shakespeare probably more authentically with us than at any time since the seventeenth century.

NOTES

1. In *Selected Essays, 1917–1932* (London: Faber & Faber, 1932), 141–6.

2. Stoll's position is concisely stated in the opening chapter of his *Art and Artifice in Shakespeare* (Cambridge: The University Press, 1934).

3. T. S. Eliot, "Shakespearean Criticism: From Dryden to Coleridge," in *A Companion to Shakespearean Studies*, H. Granville-Barker and G. B. Harrison, eds. (Cambridge: The University Press, 1946), 297.

4. A. C. Harbage, *As They Liked It* (New York: Macmillan, 1947), 112–13.

5. John Palmer, *Political Characters of Shakespeare* (London: Macmillan, 1945), viii.

6. G. Wilson Knight, *The Wheel of Fire*, 4th edition (London: Methuen, 1949), 13.

7. L. Abercrombie, "A Plea for the Liberty of Interpreting," *Proceedings of the British Academy* (1930), 163.

8. T. S. Eliot, "Introduction" to G. Wilson Knight, *The Wheel of Fire*, xxix.

9. R. B. Heilman, *This Great Stage* (Baton Rouge: Louisiana State University Press, 1948), 12.

10. *Ibid.*, 252.

11. Maud Bodkin, *Archetypal Patterns in Poetry* (London: Oxford University Press, 1934), 4.

Part II

PRINCIPLES AND METHODS

Planning

As WE READ Dr. Roberts' essay, "A New Disease," we are never in any doubt that she is presenting an argument—that is, attempting to shape our thoughts and attitudes by placing before us a selection of propositions and evidence relevant to a given subject. There is the possibility, however remote, that this writer is misinformed, even wilfully deceitful; but as we read and drive steadily forward over a series of related ideas and supporting facts, we are certain at least of the existence of a controlled discussion whose purport we follow with ease. In part, this effect of clarity is the result of precise expression: apt choice of words, careful phrasing, good sentence and paragraph structure. But more fundamentally it is the result of good planning—the disciplined selection and ordering of material in advance of composition. And here, as in all aspects of essay writing, certain principles are at work whose aim is to ensure successful communication between writer and reader. If Dr. Roberts was not conscious of following these principles in the preparation of her essay, this is only to say that the experienced writer, like the concert pianist, ceases to be aware of many of the skills which he does in fact employ. The student writer must accept the hard task of learning the rules for disciplined argument and of applying them thoughtfully in his work.

Acknowledging the fact that "A New Disease" is, of its kind, a well-written essay, we may deduce from it two basic principles of planning. First there is the dual principle of limitation and completeness—more explicitly, of completeness in discussion within limited boundaries. Dr. Roberts, accepting the limitation dictated by her topic, writes exclusively about blindness in premature babies; if any other disease or any other subject is brought into the discussion, it is introduced only in so far as it is related to the central subject of retrolental fibroplasia. Less obvious, but still important to the writing of a good essay, is another form of limitation: that the writer does not undertake to discuss the chosen subject either generally or exhaustively. A full study of retrolental fibroplasia would doubtless occupy several hundred pages. Dr. Roberts, properly following the tradition of the short essay (cf. Fr. *essayer*: to try, attempt), sets herself certain limited objectives: to give the reader a few facts about the nature of the "new disease"; to arouse his interest—perhaps even to alarm him slightly—over its high and curious incidence; to make him wonder at the enigma of its cause and at the powerlessness of modern medicine to cope with it. Yet if these are limited objectives they are at the same time objectives carefully chosen and clearly defined. We return, then, to our conception of the essay as disciplined argument. And since limitation is identifiable with disciplined argument, it is not difficult to see where the idea of completeness comes in. Though Dr. Roberts' discussion of blindness in premature babies is limited, we nevertheless derive from it a sense of "wholeness": on the one hand we detect no irrelevancies; on the other hand, content to accept the boundaries she has set, we feel that her discussion has been sufficiently extensive and that her aims have been adequately fulfilled.

To sense completeness is to sense the sum of parts properly selected and disposed. We are satisfied with the "wholeness" of the argument in "A New Disease" because we recognize that the subject (which is retrolental fibroplasia) has been nicely broken down into component parts which are severally concerned with aspects of the disease in question, and that this subject has been, as it were, laid out before our eyes in the form of an intelligible sequence of thoughts. Plainly, if we set aside for a moment the problem of order, success here is the result of the accurate division of a whole into parts. Our second principle of planning, then, is the principle of division.

To see more particularly how this dividing of a subject into parts works out in practice, we have only to proceed backwards from the completed essay, "A New Disease," to the plan of which it is the full expression. Dr. Roberts obviously conceived of four main divisions to her argument. Her first three paragraphs she devotes to establishing the fact that a new disease of blindness in premature babies has made its appearance; and in the course of setting up this division of her argument she notes that the disease has a characteristic pathology, that it is truly a "new" disease, that its incidence is widespread, and that it is unmistakably linked with prematurity. In the fourth paragraph she turns to the second main division of her argument. Here she is concerned with the proposition that the cause of the disease is entirely unknown. Since this is really the core of her argument (though the two remaining sections are needed to fill out its implications), she devotes considerable attention (four paragraphs) to making it firm: she notes that the cause cannot be proved to lie in pre-natal disturbances, that it cannot be attributed to the rigours of post-natal life faced by the premature baby, and that, recent suggestions to the contrary, it cannot be conclusively identified as virus infection. The eighth paragraph discloses the opening out of the third main division of Dr. Roberts' argument: "For the established disease no cure has been found"; and the remainder of this long paragraph she commits to marshalling evidence in support of this contention. The topic sentence of the ninth paragraph introduces the fourth main division of argument by affirming that this new disease "illustrates many of the difficulties encountered in medical research." The space devoted to this unit of thought is slight, but the proposition gains weight, at once from its terminal position and from the fact that it is a logical "capping" to the core thoughts of the two preceding divisions. In all this it will be noticed that the principle of division applies not only to the subject of the essay as a whole but also, in turn, to the main parts into which the subject has been divided. As already indicated, the opening division of "A New Disease" is made up of four subordinate units of thought (pathology, "newness," incidence, probability) which together define retrolental fibroplasia. Corresponding subdivisions are to be found within each of the other main divisions of the essay.

Here, then, is a subject satisfactorily divided into component parts. To observe a single and relatively simple example of good planning, of course, is only a small step towards acquiring the skill, and, obliged to write an essay on the character of Macbeth or on colonialism in the twentieth century, the student may still be at a loss to know how to find a succession of main ideas which will effectively outline the course of an argument. There is no easy solution to the problem; for at this point we come up against nothing less than the whole subject of logic, with its host of related studies in analysis and synthesis, in axiom and hypothesis, in proof and inference. Still, we have been able to observe the application of two important principles of planning to a specific task, and we are at least in a position to define our goal: an argument which is limited yet complete and which is suitably divided into component units of thought.

Having now covered, in the course of our analysis, the whole of the main argument and much of the subordinate argument of "A New Disease," it will be profitable to pause for a moment in order to see how the entire content of the essay can be represented in terms of a formal plan.

A New Disease

I. A new disease of blindness in premature babies has appeared.
   A. This disease has a distinctive pathology.
   B. It is truly "new."
   C. Its incidence is widespread.
   D. The probability of its occurrence varies directly with the degree of prematurity.

II. The cause of this new disease is entirely unknown.
   A. It is unlikely that it lies in pre-natal disturbances.
   B. It is unlikely that it lies in the post-natal rigours of life faced by the premature baby.
      1. It does not lie in premature exposure to light or in oxygen deficiency.
      2. Prematurity has only recently produced evidence of this disease.
   C. It is possible, but by no means certain, that it lies in virus infection.

III. For the established disease no cure has been found.
   A. Surgery and radiotherapy have proved unsuccessful.
   B. The use of A.C.T.H. has proved only partially successful.
   C. The surest check known is simply to prevent prematurity.
   D. Research continues.

IV. This new disease illustrates the problems faced by medical research.
   A. It reminds us of the complexity of the disease-process.
   B. It reminds us of the enigma of the genesis of disease.
   C. It demonstrates the dynamic nature of the struggle between medical science and nature.

With the complete plan of "A New Disease" before us, we may consider next three principles which should govern organization within the plan and which are, in fact, corollaries of the two main principles discussed above. These subsidiary principles are really principles of reasoning which are of particular force in planning. To discuss them briefly is as close as we can come in these pages to broaching the complex science of logic already referred to as the only sure guide to the suitable division of a subject into component units of thought.

An examination of the essay plan adduced from "A New Disease" will show that the main headings (I, II, III, IV) provide for divisions of thought which are mutually exclusive. This is to say simply that when Dr. Roberts is discussing one aspect of her subject she is indeed discussing one that is recognizably separate from the others: to speak of the cure for a disease, for example, is to speak of something manifestly different from its cause. When, therefore, we describe the essay as being made up of "component units of thought," we mean units of thought whose boundaries touch but do not (except for deliberate purposes of transition and emphasis) overlap. Putting it another way, we mean that all ideas presented within a given unit of argument are relevant to that unit alone, and hence would be considered irrelevant if introduced under another main heading—as would be the case, for example, if Dr. Roberts had concluded the section of her essay assigned to the causes of the "new disease" with a consideration of the unsuccessful use of A.C.T.H. as a remedy. The student, then, must learn to divide accurately. Given as a text Shakespeare's *Antony and Cleopatra*, and as a topic "The Character of Antony," he must train himself to see that the headings THE ROMAN ANTONY and THE EGYPTIAN ANTONY are accurately formulated, whereas the headings ANTONY'S POWERS OF LEADERSHIP and ANTONY'S RELATIONS WITH ENOBARBUS are not.

A second aid to reasoning out a plan lies in the principle of subordination. We can scarcely say that the headings ANTONY'S POWERS OF LEADERSHIP and ANTONY'S RELATIONS WITH ENOBARBUS are not mutually exclusive without noting that the first heading properly subsumes the second: Antony's powers of leadership are demonstrated in many ways, but perhaps in no way more forcefully than in his relations with Enobarbus. And if we accept as another major division of our discussion of Antony's character the heading WHAT OTHERS SAY ABOUT ANTONY, we shall no doubt draw upon Enobarbus a second time, adding his testimony to the testimony of Cleopatra, Caesar, Pompey, and others, as furthering by particular evidence the general consideration. Illustration is even clearer if we return to Dr. Roberts' essay. Here we see that the main headings are in fact generalizations, each of which is dependent for its authority upon a body of subordinate and supporting evidence. In the fourth paragraph, for example, the writer affirms that the cause of the disease is entirely unknown; and in the passages which follow she brings together such material (doubtless scattered in the stage prior to planning) as is likely to induce the reader to accept her contention. The material is rightly called subordinate because no part of it—the consideration of pre-natal disturbances, for instance—exists independently; instead, each finds its sole justification in the force it can lend to a general proposition. The student, then, must learn to distinguish between main argument and subordinate argument. He must train himself to see, first, that an essay on "The Character of Antony" must as a whole present a contention or thesis which, however complex its qualifications, is conclusively shaped to a certain end (Antony, say, is warm-hearted, courageous, but irresponsible), and that this end is to be reached by an orderly progress through a series of generalizations relevant to the subject; secondly, that these generalizations, which are themselves subservient to the total effect sought for in the essay, must each in turn receive the support of subordinate argument; thirdly, that any part of this subordinate argument may in its turn require support from argument subordinate to it; and so on, if need be, down the scale.

The third and final aid to reasoning out a plan lies in the principle of logical sequence. In purely expository or descriptive essays the sequence to be followed is usually predetermined by the nature of the subject itself and presents no problem; we must, for example, tell the reader how to lay the foundations for a house before we tell him how to build the walls. In the essay of contention or thesis, on the other hand, the problem of order can be extremely complex—as an analysis of Mr. Winch's essay on the universities will forcibly show. However, for present purposes it will be advisable to consider only the moderately difficult problem of order and its solution. "A New Disease," which is short and contains a relatively simple argument, is again a useful source of illustration.

Specifically, the order in which the four main thoughts of this essay are advanced is consonant with what we may call good sense or reason. Thus it seems fitting that Dr. Roberts should first give us a sufficient number of facts about the pathology, incidence, etc., of the new disease to enable us to have a firm idea of what is meant by the term "retrolental fibroplasia"; that she should then deal with the known causes of the disease, next with attempted cures; and that she should reserve for the final place in her essay a line of argument which draws out of her subject (retrolental fibroplasia) the special "message" she wishes to convey: that for modern medicine, despite its great advances, both the genesis of disease and the disease-process itself remain something of a mystery and a challenge to research. Now, given this particular group of component thoughts, we should almost certainly be disturbed by any ordering of them other than that with which Dr. Roberts has in fact confronted us. We should certainly object were she to discuss the cures for a disease for which we had no definition; and we should certainly be confused were she to write of the enigmas still faced by modern medicine *before* presenting her negative report on the remedies tentatively proposed for the "new disease." (A forecast of her concluding contention is, it is true, a possibility for the opening paragraph of her essay.)

The considerations which determine reasonable order are, of course, numerous; and frequently they are very subtle. Order in time is one such consideration—the most obvious and perhaps the most fundamental one. Dr. Roberts' discussion of the causes of the "new disease" properly precedes her discussion of remedies because any remedy which is proposed without a careful study having been made of what is causing a disease is, as we say, "unscientific" and scarcely worth serious consideration. Less obviously—and also less inevitably—in an essay on "The Character of Antony" the section devoted to THE EGYPTIAN ANTONY may well precede the section on THE ROMAN ANTONY since the Antony of Egypt and Cleopatra is the Antony we are first introduced to in the play—therefore the central Antony, it could be argued, in terms of dramatic action. But here we must part company with formula. For the same consideration of order in time may lead us to see Antony's Roman life as the main course, his Egyptian life as a deviation, and hence justify a sequence of argument which places THE ROMAN ANTONY before THE EGYPTIAN ANTONY. Considerations other than that of time will, in fact, by this point be apparent—considerations which call for movement from particular to general, from general to particular, from near to far, from less important to more important, from more important to less important, and so on. And individual cases alone can determine which of these considerations is to have sway at any given moment. Yet whatever consideration is held to be dominant the effects secured must be those of progression and suitable emphasis. If, for instance, the thesis, or part of the thesis, of our essay on "The Character of Antony" is that Antony deviates from the proper course of his life to the flesh-pots of Egypt, then we must ask ourselves whether our intention will be best served in terms both of progression (that is, a moving forward or building of argument) and of emphasis (that is, an elevation of the desired thought into relief) by accepting the order THE ROMAN ANTONY and THE EGYPTIAN ANTONY. Perhaps it will. But prescription cannot be rigid; for, in the essay, concluding place is generally emphatic place, and we could quite justifiably plan to dispose of deviation first, reserving for the final phase of the discussion what we should choose to call the central Antony of Rome.

Such pursuit of hypothetical cases soon becomes unprofitable. Since, indeed, thought and how thought is arranged are in the end inseparable, solutions to the problem of order in planning reflect in their number the almost infinite variety and complexity of which human thought is capable. All that can be urged here is that the student must plan for such an ordering of thought in his essay as will ensure a steady and systematic movement of the reader's mind from one phase of argument forward to the next and a recognition that suitable emphasis has been given, in the parts as in the whole, to major contentions. Ideas and facts dispersed at random must be made into a composition—a term appropriate, it should be recalled, to music, architecture, and painting as well as to essay writing. The student essay, whatever its subject, should be characterized by just that apparently inevitable ordering which identifies the work of a good craftsman in any of the arts.

The Paragraph

A PARAGRAPH is a group of sentences designed to develop a single unit of thought. In the essay the function of the paragraph is to present, illustrate, or modify an idea or a group of ideas corresponding to a section, subsection, or even smaller component of the essay plan. Being sufficiently long and complex for adequate statement, and yet well ordered and brief enough for ready comprehension, the paragraph is an arrangement of material which helps the reader to understand some phase of an argument or to assimilate a collection of details. The indentation of the first line of the paragraph is a signal that one unit of thought has been completed and that a new unit of thought is about to be presented.

The paragraph has a dual character: it is an essay in miniature, endowed with some measure of individuality, composed of related material, and as carefully designed as the essay itself; but it is also an integral part of the composition in which it stands. Hence, the paragraph cannot be fully studied without reference to the whole essay. Nevertheless, it will be necessary to concentrate attention on the paragraph as an independent unit if we are to understand the mechanics of its construction. As it happens, the two areas of discussion overlap: for example, the principles of completeness, limitation, and division, which, as we have seen, regulate the proper disposition of an argument during the planning stage of an essay, are equally relevant to a just ordering of material in the paragraph.

In accordance with the principle of completeness within limited boundaries, each paragraph should deal with only one main idea, and that idea should be developed only to the point where it fulfils both the writer's over-all and his immediate purpose. In the final paragraph of her essay, Dr. Roberts discusses one point and one point only: that the new disease of retrolental fibroplasia illustrates many of the difficulties faced in medical research. In her selection of the illustrations themselves she shows discrimination and a sense of economy—doubtless many examples other than the ones she finally chose came to mind as she planned her essay, but were rejected because a long catalogue would have overloaded, and so thrown off balance, that part of her argument. The three problems

she names, on the other hand, are significant and intriguing enough
to catch the reader's attention, to bring the composition itself to an
impressive conclusion, and, above all, to establish beyond doubt the
justness of the contention which is the motivating idea of the paragraph. Had she given way to the temptation to present at the same
time, perhaps most entertainingly, a comparison between the problems of modern and nineteenth-century research, the paragraph, and
with it the whole framework of her argument, would have collapsed
under the conflict of stresses. Again, in her third paragraph she
supplies no more than the bare minimum of statistics necessary to
establish the impression that the disease is widespread (she mentions
three continents), has assumed alarming proportions, and is on the
increase. It is essential, then, that the student should re-examine the
paragraph he has written and ask himself, first, whether he has
said all that is needed to establish his main point, and secondly,
whether he has said more than enough, either by digressing or by
overweighting some part of his discussion.

Singleness of purpose within the paragraph, however, does not
preclude the introduction of subsidiary elements which modify the
principal idea. In the penultimate paragraph of her essay, Dr.
Roberts begins by stating emphatically that no cure has yet been
found for retrolental fibroplasia. However, she goes on to indicate
the types of treatment attempted and the degree of success each has
had. "First results [of the application of A.C.T.H.]," she says, "were
indeterminate, but more recently workers in this country have
claimed some success." Perhaps a cure has in fact been found. It is
clear that this discussion of the treatments attempted has modified
the negative in the writer's major contention, and, incidentally, has
suggested the size and urgency of the doctor's problems. But it has
not deposed the major contention itself.

We have seen that, in each paragraph, we must communicate one
central idea to the reader with clarity and due emphasis. In this
task we may proceed in one of three ways: following the most
common practice, we may state our topic explicitly in one sentence;
or we may present it by implication; or we may indicate it in part
explicitly and in part by implication.

Though she makes some use of the third, Dr. Roberts obviously
prefers the first method. Her topic sentences fall with the regularity
of sharp hammer blows throughout her essay, driving home each

phase of her discussion until she has made of the whole a solid structure. Not that these blows are monotonous; this effect she avoids by varying the position of her topic sentence. In each of her last three paragraphs, for instance, she places the topic sentence at the beginning. But in the opening paragraph the topic statement is shared between the fourth and fifth sentences and is preceded by three introductory sentences which enable the reader to orient himself. Occasionally, as in the third paragraph, it is adduced at the end from the evidence paraded before it, although on this occasion it has been tentatively defined in the opening sentence, which virtually poses the question "Is retrolental fibroplasia a new disease?" Implicit presentation of the topic finds little place in Dr. Roberts' essay. This is a method of paragraph organization to be used sparingly and then only with great care taken to ensure that clarity and coherence of argument are not imperilled. The dangers of using it casually are illustrated in certain paragraphs of "The Abbey's Needs."

The basic argument of an essay can be identified by examining the sequence of topic sentences in the successive paragraphs. In itself, such a bare-bones sequence of ideas is not likely either to convince or to interest us—the one-sentence paragraph is normally ineffective. The writer will convince us only if he supports the central idea of each paragraph with testimony which establishes its validity, and he will interest us only if he presents this testimony in systematic and attractive form. What he selects will be determined very much by his own knowledge, tastes, and expository powers, but he must take into account the knowledge, tastes, and powers of comprehension of his reader. (Dr. Roberts doubtless felt obliged again and again to restrain an interest in medical technicalities as much because her audience would lack either ability or inclination to follow her explanations as because elaboration would have destroyed the balance and tone of her essay.) How the writer presents his material will be governed largely by the demands of expediency—by the particular purpose he has in mind.

It will be profitable at this point to set down the commonest methods of advancing the argument of a paragraph. Nearly all are variants of one or other of two basic methods of procedure which are fundamental to all thinking: enumeration, and comparison and contrast. The former is operative in any listing of illustrations or supporting detail, in any attempt at classification, and in any consideration of causes and effects. The latter method, which establishes similarities or differences between objects or ideas, may take the form of definition (for a statement of the precise nature of an object or idea entails a recognition of its differentiae), elimination (that is, an explicit rejection of whatever is inapplicable to the item under consideration), or analogy. In only the simplest of discussions, however, can the argument within a paragraph be handled by a single method. More often than not various methods are used in combination. The more elaborate the chain of thought, or the more numerous and diverse the details within a paragraph, the more varied and subtle the structure is likely to be.

An effective paragraph is like the skilfully erected wall of a house and demands in its construction care very similar to that given by the builder. In the first place, the paragraph must show an orderly disposition and logical development of ideas, an end easily gained if the essay plan represents an argument fully considered to the last detail, and if the requirements of completeness and limitation have been met in every part of it. In the second place, sentences and phrases must be firmly yet unobtrusively cemented together throughout the paragraph. Cohesion of this sort is achieved mainly by the use of transitional sentences, phrases, and words, by the substitution of pronouns for nouns, and by the repetition of ideas, which, like synonymy and the repetition of key words, is an important means of providing emphasis and of showing clearly the direction of an argument. In the third place, the writer must guard against capricious changes in point of view—changes in the tense, mood, or voice of verbs, or in the person or number of pronouns. In particular, the casual shift from "one" to "you" or from "we" to "I," which so often characterizes everyday conversation, has no place in essay writing, where, to be admissible, any alteration of point of view should fulfil a definite purpose. The safeguard here is careful revision.

It has been pointed out that since the paragraph is in a sense an essay in miniature, it cannot be studied without reference to neighbouring paragraphs and to the essay of which it is an integral part. Mr. Henn's essay, "The Canadian Dilemma," exemplifies this point. The core of the argument is an attempt to account for Canadian resentment of the United States. To this Mr. Henn devotes Paragraphs 5 to 8, each of which is informed by a single main idea, but all of which are interdependent. In the first of these he contends that, before a nation can attain a sense of national identity, at least one of three conditions must be present, and that Canada lacks all three. The next paragraph parallels this one by exploring in the same order each of these prerequisites, though Canada's inability to realize the first two conditions is now made the cause of her inability to realize the third—hence the Canadian tendency to turn "to the past in search of a more substantial creed." To this combination of circumstances, Mr. Henn, in the following two paragraphs, attributes the resentment of both English-Canadians and French-Canadians against the United States. Whether he is completely justified here in making two paragraphs where one would have served is open to question—in his support it may be argued that the paragraph division subtly accentuates the split between the two racial groups and at the same time enables the writer to drive home their common fear of the American way of life. At all events, we must admit that the argument presented in these paragraphs is easy to follow and convincing. Nor is this success merely the result of a careful selection and presentation of material within each paragraph, for it is clear that the author has also given careful attention to the coherence of the section as a whole. There is no irrelevancy, no overlapping of ideas, no unnecessary repetition of expressions, no obvious omission, no major shift in point of view, no interruption of the dispassionate and systematic manner by decorative flourishes.

Coherence here is based on the logic of the argument. But a further analysis of Mr. Henn's essay shows that coherence is also a matter of the skilful use of transitional words and phrases which prescribe boundaries, make connections, and mark shifts in emphasis. In the fifth paragraph, for example, returning to the theme of resentment mentioned near the beginning of his essay, Mr. Henn chooses the phrase "more subtle analysis," which establishes a connection with the preceding stage of the discussion and points the way to the nature of the discussion to follow. The fifth and sixth paragraphs are linked by the words "Canada" (the last word of the fifth paragraph) and "The country" (the first words of the sixth paragraph), and by the parallel structure of the main argument of each. In the seventh, "Considered against this background" emphasizes a relation with the sixth, and, indeed, with the fifth, in which this major phase of the argument originated. The eighth paragraph attaches itself to the seventh with the aid of "similarly," a word that warns the reader to expect a parallel argument. The first sentence of almost every paragraph of the essay contains the word "Canada" or "Canadian."

Handled with such dexterity, connectives clearly but unobtrusively chart the reader's route through a maze of argument. Yet if a writer overworks devices of this nature, or uses them too mechanically, the pace of his essay will flag, and with it the reader's attention. Variety is important. What, for example, could be duller than the constant chiming of the same structure in sentence after sentence, or the steady repetition of an elementary paragraph structure in which example follows topic sentence as surely as the clanging of a bell follows each stroke of its clapper? It is common for writers to rely almost instinctively upon a small stock of favourite expressions and forms. In the first draft of an essay, such repetitions are pardonable, but not in the finished essay, from which all such blemishes should have been removed.

It may be asked what correspondence exists between the number of paragraphs in an essay and the number of units of thought, main and subordinate, defined in the essay plan. A comparison of Dr. Roberts' essay with the plan on page 52 reveals that the author used nine paragraphs to cover the four main divisions of the plan: two embody the whole of the last two sections, whereas four are devoted to the second section alone; and, of these latter, two deal with a single subsection of the argument. Plainly the correspondence is slight. And the reason for this fact is that the essayist, in the preparation of a plan, is an architect rather than a builder. An architect, having formed his idea of a house and embodied this idea in notes and drawings, leaves to the builder the translation of these into a material structure. Similarly, the essayist grapples in his plan with the problems of the order and relative importance of ideas, but, since some ideas require more elucidation than others, he does not commit himself to how many paragraphs should be allotted to each section. Nor does he commit himself to the number or even the nature of the illustrations to be incorporated in the essay. In none but the simplest of discussions are the contents of each paragraph likely to coincide with the divisions and subdivisions of the plan.

One aspect of paragraph writing has yet to be discussed. It concerns the vexed problem of opening and closing an essay. There is a widespread belief that an essay should always begin with an

"Introduction"—a receptacle for amusing anecdotes, autobiographical curiosities, expressions of enthusiasm for the subject, or apologies for the inadequate scholarship displayed in the pages to follow. All such opening gambits are apparently intended to dispose the reader more favourably towards the writer. Another widespread belief is that an opening paragraph is the place either for a restatement of the essay title or for a mechanical paragraph-by-paragraph forecast of the course likely to be taken by the argument. It is often thought, too, that a concluding paragraph is a kind of appendage and provides an appropriate occasion for the broadest of generalizations and the most extravagant of rhetorical flourishes. Finally, it is often thought that between the "Introduction" and the "Conclusion" lies an area to be designated "Main Body of Essay." Such views are far removed from the truth.

The "main body" of an essay is the essay itself, every element of which must contribute to the total and unified impression intended by its author. An argument must have a beginning, but that is the *terminus a quo* prescribed by the first main section of the plan. It must also have an ending, but that is the *terminus ad quem* prescribed by the last main section of the plan. Important though it is that the writer should engage the reader's attention from the outset, it is still more important that he should come immediately to grips with the topic proposed in his title. He should then retain his control over discussion and reader alike up to and including the final paragraph, in which he should end as vigorously as he began. As he concludes, he may gain some advantage by a discreet intensification of expression. A style slightly more emphatic than usual may help to close firmly, but not to slam, the door on his argument. Literary graces, indeed, unlike wild and empty rhetorical gestures, are not to be excluded from this or any other paragraph; properly employed, they are harnessed to the essay writer's single purpose—to communicate, as clearly and as convincingly as possible, a logical sequence of thoughts.

The Sentence

SINCE THE VERY MENTION of the word *sentence* in the present context is likely to conjure up immediately the formidable subject of grammar, it will be well at the outset to state plainly that grammar will receive little attention in this chapter. There are reasons for this decision. To begin with, grammar is too big a subject to treat adequately in the space at our disposal: Otto Jesperson's *A Modern English Grammar*, certainly the most satisfactory study in this field, runs to seven volumes for a total of 3,593 pages. Secondly, it is a subject that can legitimately be omitted from a book which is concerned specifically and exclusively with the undergraduate essay. Universities assume that undergraduates have the competence to write grammatical sentences, and they are not prepared to provide instruction for those who lack this competence. There is a third reason and, for our purposes, an important one. Too much attention to grammar may well obscure the value of two other subjects which also must be mastered if the student is to write good prose. A mastery of grammar ensures that our sentences will be technically correct; it does not ensure that they will be either clear or effective. To be clear, sentences must be so constructed that the ideas they contain are logically related—we must, therefore, direct attention to the study of logic. To be effective, sentences must be so constructed that certain ideas are emphasized while other ideas are given only incidental notice—we must, therefore, direct attention to the study of rhetoric. In this discussion, we shall assume a knowledge of grammar and concentrate attention on problems involving logical relationship and emphasis.

Grammar is basic, but it is not enough. The following sentences (adapted from the opening sentence of Mr. Henn's "The Canadian Dilemma") are grammatically correct but they are, respectively, nonsensical and confused:

Since they have not as yet been made the recipients of Marshall Aid, it is more than a little surprising to discover that Canadians have reacted quite as violently as any left-wing European to the post-war shift in dress design which has made France once again the dominant nation in the world of fashion.

Though they have not as yet been made the recipients of Marshall Aid, it is more than a little surprising to discover that Canadians have reacted as violently as any left-wing European to the post-war shift in world power which has made the United States the economically dominant nation of Western civilization.

On the other hand, it is possible to write a sentence which is both clear and effective, but which is also ungrammatical:

Since they have not as yet been made the recipients of Marshall Aid, it is more than a little surprising to discover that Canadians has reacted quite as violently as any left-wing European to the post-war shift in world power which has made the United States the economically dominant nation of Western civilization.

Our reaction to this ungrammatical sentence is quite definite: we understand what is being said, but we feel that the writer is either careless or illiterate—careless if "Canadians has" is a single slip in an otherwise impeccable stretch of prose, illiterate if errors such as this one chronically disfigure his sentences. If we feel that he is illiterate or careless, our attitude towards the writer will be unfavourable and we shall be indisposed to accept his ideas. But we should note that the grammatical error does not necessarily interfere with our receipt of the ideas presented. It is one thing to reject a man's ideas on the ground that his manner of expressing them raises doubts as to his right to be considered an authority; it is quite another to reject his ideas because we have no clear understanding of what he is trying to say.

To reassert the importance of logic and rhetoric and to place them on a parity with grammar as two of the three basic elements in good English prose is to return to the approach which governed the teaching of English composition at the time of its beginnings in the sixteenth century and for three hundred years thereafter. During the Middle Ages, the study of Latin prose composition (a basic subject, since Latin was the language of instruction in all advanced studies) had included the study of grammar, logic, and rhetoric: the student had first learned how to write a correct sentence; next, how to write a logical series of sentences (the paragraph); finally, how to present a convincing argument (the essay). The first teachers of English composition adapted to the teaching of the new language the methods they had been using in the teaching of the old; for example, they stressed as vigorously as did the grammarians, logicians, and rhetoricians of the fourteenth century the classical principles of unity, coherence, and emphasis. Grammar became separated from logic and rhetoric in the nineteenth century; with the introduction of mass education, grammar, always the basic subject, became a subject for the schools, while logic and rhetoric gravitated to the universities. An emphasis on logic and rhetoric is, therefore, appropriate in a book designed for university students. However, since logical and rhetorical effects are normally the result of structural arrangement, we must begin with a reference to grammar.

GRAMMAR

The preceding chapters on "Planning" and "The Paragraph" have emphasized the principle of unity. Both the sound essay and the sound paragraph, it has been argued, are organic wholes, whose parts, though detachable for purposes of analysis, are so intermeshed that their separate identities are lost in the final product. The sentence, too, has its detachable parts—clauses; and these, like the sentences within the paragraph, and like the paragraphs within the essay, are amenable to independent analysis. Technically, the process can be carried further: clauses contain words and phrases, phrases contain words, words contain letters. But we must notice a significant change that occurs when the analysis is undertaken below the level of the sentence. The sentence, though a part of a paragraph, has an independent identity; it is, at its own level, a complete communication. The paragraph, though a part of an essay, is also a self-contained unit; it, too, is a complete communication. But, unless the clause is itself a sentence (that is, an independent clause), it is not a complete communication. There is no complete communication in the subordinate clause:

> When the moon shines;

or in the phrase:

> Over the mountain;

or in the word:

> I.

But the sentence is a complete and independent communication:

> When the moon shines over the mountain, I'll be waiting
> at the kitchen door.

The sentence stands by itself; unlike the word, phrase, or subordinate clause, it has an immediate significance that is independent of what precedes or follows. It is at one and the same time the basis for the larger elements, since the paragraph and hence the essay presuppose the sentence, and also the basis for the smaller elements, since words, phrases, and subordinate clauses achieve formal significance when, and only when, they are presented in the context of the complete sentence. Thus the sentence occupies a unique position in the hierarchy of compositional elements—it is the basic unit of communication. Two important implications derive from this fact.

First, to say that the parts of a sentence depend for their formal significance on the whole sentence is to say that the meaning of a word, phrase, or subordinate clause is in some way modified—and at times radically—by the context. As an example of radical modification, take the word *hand*:

> The *hand* that rocks the cradle rules the world.
> I have three aces in my *hand*.
> I have three apples in my *hand*.
> Give me a *hand* with this table.

But—and this is the second implication—the dependence of part on whole has as its corollary the dependence of whole on part. The slightest change alters the meaning of the sentence: the change of a letter—

> When the moon shines over the mountain, I'll be wailing
> at the kitchen door,

the addition of a phrase—

> He is in excellent health.
> He is in excellent health—for a man of ninety,

the ordering of the words—

> I have *only* one friend.
> I *only* have one friend.
> *Only* I have one friend.

Thus part is determined by whole, and whole is determined by part. Are we, then, simply going around in circles? No: we are discovering that relationship is the crucial fact in the sentence—the relation of part to whole and of whole to part. Grammar is the subject which deals with the relations of words in sentences; hence its fundamental importance. As we shall see, it is by arranging our ideas in the appropriate grammatical structure that we ensure that our ideas are logically related and effectively presented.

Logic

Grammatically, sentences may be divided into four main types according to the number and nature of the clauses present. A simple sentence contains one main or independent clause, a compound sentence contains two or more main clauses, a complex sentence contains one main clause and one or more subordinate clauses. The compound-complex sentence combines the characteristics of the last two types—two or more main clauses and one or more subordinate clauses.

The simple sentence enjoys the advantages that go with simplicity. The idea which is expressed in a simple sentence stands out more clearly than it would were it combined with a second idea in a compound or complex sentence. If we gave a value of 100 to each sentence, the three basic types could be thus represented:

Simple	IDEA A (100)	.	
Compound	IDEA A (50)	, and	IDEA B (50)
Complex	IDEA A (main clause) (75),		IDEA B (subordinated) (25).

or

IDEA A (subordinated) (25),	IDEA B (main clause) (75).

The idea expressed in a simple sentence will not stand out clearly if it is one of a series of ideas similarly expressed. The particular effectiveness of the simple sentence depends upon contrast, as does the particular effectiveness of the short paragraph.

There are disadvantages as well as advantages in simplicity. Because it contains a single clause, the simple sentence is restricted in its capacity to express complicated ideas. Furthermore, it is limited to a single type of structural variation, that provided by *voice*:

> Claudius is troubled by Hamlet's actions.
> Hamlet's actions trouble Claudius.

In terms of logic, there is nothing to choose between these two sentences. There is, however, something to choose between them in terms of rhetoric. In the first example, where the passive voice is used, we begin with Claudius and end with Hamlet's actions; in the second, we begin with Hamlet's actions (or with Hamlet) and we end with Claudius. So much for the simple sentence.

The compound sentence is also restricted in its structural possibilities, in this case by the fact that the clauses must be co-ordinated. Logically, all compound sentences of two clauses fall into the same pattern:

IDEA A (50)	, and	IDEA B (50) .
The Collegiate Church of St. Peter in Westminster has been eight hundred and eighty-eight years in the building,		and it is not finished yet.

However, there are two methods of signalling co-ordination within the sentence. The first, exemplified above, is by the use of a co-ordinating conjunction (*and, but, or, so, for, nor*). The second is by use of the semicolon:

The Collegiate Church of St. Peter in Westminster has been eight hundred and eighty-eight years in the building; it is not finished yet.

Here, the ideas are simply juxtaposed, as they would be if they were placed in separate sentences:

The Collegiate Church of St. Peter in Westminster has been eight hundred and eighty-eight years in the building. It is not finished yet.

Placed in separate sentences, the independence of the two ideas is stressed. The semicolon suggests their *inter*dependence though less strongly than does the comma, which is the punctuation mark normally used when the ideas are related by a co-ordinating conjunction:

The Collegiate Church of St. Peter in Westminster has been eight hundred and eighty-eight years in the building, and it is not finished yet.

The nature of the relationship between the co-ordinated ideas can be indicated in the semicolon construction if a conjunctive adverb is used—*hence, yet, therefore, however,* etc.

The Collegiate Church of St. Peter in Westminster has been eight hundred and eighty-eight years in the building; however, it is not finished yet.

Conjunctive adverbs, like co-ordinating conjunctions and prepositions, are what modern linguists call "function words"—words which denote relationship. Such words are difficult to define, but their meaning is remarkably constant, far more constant than the meaning of nouns, verbs, adjectives, and adverbs. A word like *hand*, as we have seen, can have many meanings—the *Oxford English Dictionary* records no less than fifty-nine. But a word like *and* or *nevertheless* has a single fixed meaning. The function words are emotionless words; entirely denotative in character, they carry no association or undertones. They conduct their business of indicating the relation that other words bear to each other without attracting attention to themselves. Because they are signposts which give specific instructions, they must be used with scrupulous care. *And* sends the reader down one path; *but* or *for* down an entirely different path. No error—and it will be an error of logic, not of grammar—is more serious than the use of the wrong conjunction or conjunctive adverb.

When we turn to the complex sentence, the possibilities for structural variation are further extended, for now subordination is introduced. Idea A can be subordinated to Idea B or—with slight variation of phrasing—Idea B can be subordinated to Idea A. Thus:

Though the Collegiate Church of St. Peter in Westminster has been eight hundred and eighty-eight years in the building,	it is not finished yet.

But also:

Though the Collegiate Church of St. Peter in Westminster is still not finished,	it has been eight hundred and eighty-eight years in the building.

There are other possibilities:

The Collegiate Church of St. Peter in Westminster, which has been eight hundred and eighty-eight years in the building, is not finished yet.

When the complex sentence contains three clauses, the permutations and combinations increase accordingly. Idea A or Idea B or Idea C can be the main clause; if idea A is the main clause, both Idea B and Idea C can be subordinated to it, or Idea B can be subordinated to Idea A and Idea C subordinated to Idea B, or Idea C can be subordinated to Idea B and Idea B subordinated to Idea C. And so on. Two examples will suffice:

The Collegiate Church of St. Peter in Westminster is not likely ever to be finished, since it has been eight hundred and eighty-eight years in the building and it is still not finished.

Since the Cathedral Church of St. Peter in Westminster remains unfinished though it has been eight hundred and eighty-eight years in the building, it can be regarded as perpetually under construction.

With the compound-complex sentence, which introduces co-ordination and subordination, the possible variations extend still further. For example, . . . but surely we have made our point.

The point is that the structural resources of the sentence are almost unlimited. If we are concerned with five ideas, we can express them in one sentence or in two or in three or in four or in five. We can isolate, co-ordinate, subordinate. Furthermore, by drawing on the rich storehouse of co-ordinate and subordinate conjunctions and of conjunctive adverbs, we can define the exact relationship which exists between our ideas: cause and effect, order in time, duration, location in space, degree of importance, conditionality, and many more. Since the structure of our language and the resources of our vocabulary combine to provide endless alternatives, we have no excuse if we fail to relate our ideas with logical precision.

RHETORIC

It has been said that 50 per cent of Hollywood plots are variations on a single theme: Boy Meets Girl, Boy Loses Girl, Boy Gets Girl. Aside from the variations that result from changing the characters and background of the individuals concerned, very different effects can be produced by shifting the emphasis among the five principal elements in the compound. Emphasis can be placed on the boy, or on the girl, or on the meeting, or on the losing, or on the getting. It is even possible to rearrange the order of events; the flashback technique makes it possible to begin at the conclusion and to end at the beginning. The formula, of course, is not an invention of Hollywood; it has been used for thousands of years by storytellers in many lands, and it has provided the base for many great poems, plays, and novels.

The essay writer enjoys comparable freedom with every sentence he writes. The ideas contained in Mr. Laird's opening sentence ("The Collegiate Church . . .") can, as we have seen, be expressed in many ways. It is true that no two alternatives produce precisely the same effect; the slightest change in any part affects the whole (*waiting, wailing*). The point is that the writer is in a position to pick and choose, and if he chooses badly he has no one to blame but himself.

There are two basic methods of adjusting emphasis in the sentence. We have already been considering the first—grammatical arrangement. The second is by varying the amount of attention devoted to each idea. The Collegiate Church can be described in different ways:

The Collegiate Church of St. Peter in Westminster, more familiar to the world still as Westminster Abbey. . . .

The Collegiate Church of St. Peter in Westminster. . . .

Westminster Abbey. . . .

We shall conclude this chapter by discussing these two methods.

Emphasis varies inversely with length. Let us examine once again the opening sentence of Mr. Laird's essay, including in it this time a phrase which has hitherto been omitted:

The Collegiate Church of St. Peter in Westminster, more familiar to the world still as Westminster Abbey, has been eight hundred and eighty-eight years in the building, and it is not finished yet.

Since the two clauses are co-ordinated, they are, in terms of logic, of equal importance. Nonetheless, it is the second clause which receives our main attention, and primarily because of its relative brevity. The shorter the clause, the more emphatic it will be—this in one principle to bear in mind. It has its obverse: the longer the clause, the less emphasis it will receive as a unit. The addition of "more familiar to the world still as Westminster Abbey" to an already lengthy clause makes it more difficult for us to see this clause as a self-contained unit; the clause which follows ("it is not finished yet") presents no such difficulty, and consequently it receives additional emphasis through the contrasting clarity of its outline.

"The longer the clause, the less emphasis it will receive *as a unit*." Increased length may, however, attract attention to an element within the clause. Mr. Laird's added phrase places the Collegiate

Church in more prominent view. The Church would be even more prominent if the sentence read:

The Collegiate Church of St. Peter in Westminster, more familiar to the world still as Westminster Abbey, and for hundreds of years the crowning place of England's kings and queens, has been eight hundred and eighty-eight years in the building, and it is not finished yet.

The question to be asked by the writer is: should the Collegiate Church receive marked attention in this sentence? He can answer the question only by weighing the rival claims of the related ideas.

The short second clause of Mr. Laird's sentence also receives special emphasis because it comes at the end of the sentence. Change this position and we have:

It is still not finished; yet the Collegiate Church of St. Peter in Westminster, more familiar to the world still as Westminster Abbey, has been eight hundred and eighty-eight years in the building.

This arrangement does not place as much emphasis on the idea contained in the shorter clause as does Mr. Laird's original. Final position tends to be the emphatic position. This principle becomes increasingly operative as the number of clauses in the series increases: final position in a series of three is more emphatic than final position in a series of two:

The Collegiate Church of St. Peter in Westminster has had many builders, it has been eight hundred and eighty-eight years in the building, and it is not finished yet.

Initial position is, of course, more emphatic than middle position.

Grammatical structure can serve the purpose of riveting our attention. Compare the above version of Mr. Laird's sentence, in which each of the three clauses is placed in the passive construction, with the following:

Many builders have worked on the Collegiate Church of St. Peter in Westminster, the church has been eight hundred and eighty-eight years in the building, and it remains unfinished.

The sentence now lacks rhythm, but also the reader is not sure on what subject his attention should be directed—on the builders or on the church. In contrast, the parallel structure of the previous version focuses attention remorselessly on the object of the writer's immediate concern: The Collegiate Church was ... it has been ... it is ....

Matthew Arnold once said that anything he repeated three times was important and that anything he repeated five times was true. He was asserting the importance of repetition as a rhetorical device. Repetition is, perhaps, the most powerful of all means of obtaining emphasis. But repetition is of the word or phrase; we seldom repeat whole sentences. For a consideration of the rhetorical effects of repetition we must turn to the following chapter on Diction.

Diction

THIS CHAPTER is about words. We must, however, continue to regard the writing of an essay as presenting an essentially unified problem in disciplined and effective communication. Problems of diction are not truly separable from problems of sentence and paragraph structure, for we cannot formulate ideas and develop an argument without being intimately concerned with choosing and ordering words. Still, the very fact that a concern for words interpenetrates all other aspects of composition demonstrates the importance of the subject and recommends it for special consideration. The discussion which follows, moreover, will indicate that the writer must accept at some stage in the revision of his essay the special responsibility of examining the choice of word he has made to communicate his meaning at any given point.

Diction may indeed be defined as *choice of words*; and faults or weaknesses in diction arise when we choose a word which is categorically wrong from the point of view of usage, or which is not needed to convey our meaning, or which is less serviceable in conveying our meaning than some other word would be. As we shall see in a moment, both the use of the categorically wrong word and the use of the unnecessary word present relatively simple problems, since both are the result of more or less arbitrary choices. But four-fifths of our difficulties with diction are caused by the fact that we must again and again make a complex and discriminating choice between words that will serve us well, words that will serve us indifferently, and words that will serve us badly. This is the challenge of all civilized languages, in which immense vocabularies designed to express every shade of thought and perception known to man have been built up over the centuries; and it is the particular challenge of the English language, which is a spectacularly rich storehouse of possible ways of saying things. We all have at our immediate disposal, of course, a stock of words and phrases which meets the needs of casual communication; and when we are required to write an essay and wish to avoid hard work we can always get something down on paper by drawing perfunctorily upon this stock to express loosely our loose thoughts on the subject in hand. If we say that Hamlet *feels badly about his mother's marriage to Claudius,* we record a truth that will pass muster as an idea. On the other hand, the truth we have thus expressed is as obvious as it is inexact, and we have gone scarcely any distance along the path of discrimination which Mr. Frame has travelled when he observes of Hamlet that *his mother's sin has tainted him.* And all along that path are countless choices to be made as we try to lodge our developing perceptions in exact and appropriate words. What shall we call Gertrude's marriage to Claudius—*misconduct, misbehaviour, delinquency,* a *vice,* an *error,* a *fault,* a *transgression,* a *lapse,* a *flaw,* or, as Mr. Frame has chosen, a *sin?* And does this *taint* Hamlet, as Mr. Frame suggests, or does it *infect, contaminate, poison, blight, defile, vitiate, debase, degrade, pervert, demoralize,* or *brutalize* him? In all this the human mind, if properly equipped and made to concentrate on its task, can operate with uncanny ingenuity and efficiency. Over two centuries ago Swift had his Lemuel Gulliver visit an imaginary island where the inhabitants had invented a machine which juggled words into books. Swift plainly thought the idea ridiculous, and he was quite right. The traffic in messages about words that goes on in our minds as we write a paragraph of closely reasoned prose makes the operations of an IBM electronic calculator while solving a difficult problem appear primitive in the extreme.

It has been suggested in the preceding paragraph that problems of diction arise mainly in connection with the choices which must be made between the less serviceable and the more serviceable word. Put another way, this means that problems of diction are not the exclusive preserve of bad or weak writers, that they are on the contrary quite "normal" and part of the process of all careful writing. The expert writer may reach a point where he is scarcely conscious of problems of paragraph and sentence structure—even of essay structure—as we have examined these formally in this book; but it is unlikely that he ever stops being acutely conscious of selecting and rejecting words a dozen times in the course of writing a paragraph. And it is with the "normal" aspect of the subject that we are here mainly concerned. However, the "abnormal" aspects—those of wrong usage and the unnecessary word—should not be dismissed without comment.

Diction which is faulty rather than weak should not be common at university level. An education in language which is begun in a childhood environment of literacy, which is continued in twelve or thirteen years of formal schooling, and which has been constantly supported by reading and listening, should have produced in the undergraduate the power to distinguish between right and wrong usage. Difficulties will arise, it is true, and vigilance will always be necessary. The student may write that Hamlet is *aggravated* by the questions asked by Rosencrantz and Guildenstern, when he means that Hamlet is *angered* or *annoyed* or *nettled*; and he may write that the Hamlet of the opening scene of the play appears *disinterested,* when he means that this figure standing apart from the other members of the court appears *indifferent to* or *uninterested in* his surroundings. And he may write *affect* when he means *effect, infer* when he means *imply, illusion* when he means *allusion.* He may even (though this is hardly to be believed) fall into the pit of incorrect usage named after Mrs. Malaprop, a character in Sheridan's *Rivals,* who, when accused of decking her "dull chat" with words she didn't understand, replied: "Sure if I reprehend anything in this world it is the use of my oracular tongue, and a nice derangement of epitaphs." But all these are more or less monumental errors. They should occur very seldom indeed in an undergraduate essay; and when they do occur they are fairly easy to detect and remedy.

The student's decision (if it can be called that) to use a word which is not needed to convey his meaning is another matter and stands closer to the central question of choice between the less serviceable and the more serviceable word. Unlike his use of the wrong word, his use of the unnecessary word does not threaten a serious breakdown in communication; nevertheless, it is a flagrant weakness and is therefore akin to the fault of wrong usage in being readily amenable to detection and remedy. Yet the superfluous word is not really a careless choice; it is usually the result of a kind of misguided conscientiousness. It is conscientiousness, for instance, in combination with a feeling of insecurity, which produces the weakness of the "double take." Thus, the student may write that Hamlet is *very much disturbed and emotionally upset* by his interview with Ophelia; and in so doing he will be reflecting an earnest desire to suggest that something drastic has happened in this scene. Because he is unsure of his resources, however, he produces, not a single solid punch, but a series of weak jabs at the object of his thought. Revising what he has written, he may decide that *emotionally* does nothing that is not covered by *disturbed* and *upset*, that *upset* overlaps with *disturbed*, and that *very much disturbed* points to the use of a more intensive word. And he may then scratch out the whole phrase and simply say that Hamlet is *tortured* or *dismayed* or *appalled* or *distressed* or *tormented* by this encounter with the woman who now rejects his love. Alternatively and doubtless still from the basis of the writer's insecurity, the superfluous word may appear in the form of a rhetorical flourish. The student, for example, may be prompted to say that there are five soliloquies, not in Shakespeare's *Hamlet*, but in Shakespeare's *famous drama Hamlet*. Finally, there is the excessive use of qualifiers, adjectival or adverbial. Here indeed it is the scrupulous rather than the careless mind that is likely to be in difficulty, for to such a mind the very richness of the English language is a temptation to modify and modify and modify yet again the meaning of a noun or verb—even of an adjective or adverb which is already drawing a load of qualification. It does not quite follow that the fewer the modifiers the better the essay, since accurate modification is obviously an essential of perceptive argument. But the student must remember that each modification entails an adjustment in sense and a consequent hesitation in the reader's flow of understanding; and he must therefore modify sparingly and always with an eye to the strict needs of his sentence. He may find himself, for instance, beginning a paragraph of an essay on Hamlet's soliloquies by writing: "The not uncommon ability to argue forcefully on both sides of a contentious moral question normally, or at any rate often, implies only a rather alert and perhaps ingenious or subtle mind. . . ." He will do better, however, to accept a version closer to Mr. Frame's: "The ability to argue on both sides of a question normally implies only an alert and ingenious mind. . . ." The simple test he will apply to reach this end will be to strike out such modifiers as might be considered dispensable and see how his sentence stands up without them. He may find that some have to be retained; but he may also find that many can be abandoned without a qualm.

Having considered the question of wrong usage and the question of the unnecessary word, we part company with what is easy to detect and remedy. The remaining problem—that of the choice which must be made when the less serviceable word jostles the more serviceable word—provides the ground on which the writer's most prolonged and arduous battles must be fought. Here, even if he is awake to his responsibilities, he can often only suspect that the word he has initially accepted is not as accurate or as appropriate as some other word might be; and to improve upon his choice he has, beyond a few general principles, no sure guide through the files of competing forms of expression other than his own intelligence applied doggedly to the task of discrimination. A dictionary will quickly dispel doubts he may have about the proper use of the word *disinterested*, and rudimentary common sense will tell him that *emotionally upset* is a redundancy. But neither of these authorities will tell him exactly how he should represent Gertrude's marriage to Claudius. A good dictionary can often help him; but often, too, it will merely involve him in a puzzling round of interchangeable entries—under *misconduct*: *misbehaviour, delinquency*; under *delinquency*: *misbehaviour, misconduct*. And rudimentary common sense will probably lead him to stay with the easy solution provided in the text's *o'erhasty marriage*. Aware that remedy is required, he will have to seek this remedy by other and harder means.

These other and harder means are more easily illustrated than described. It will often be the case, of course, and increasingly so as the writer gains mastery over his instruments, that thoughts will be formulated in such precise sequence that the right word, as Yeats said of the good poetic phrase, will fall into place with the sharp finality of the click of a latch. On the other hand, even experienced writers testify to their constant search for the right word, and the fact that they usually conduct this search with great speed and efficiency should not blind us to the complex processes involved. It will be worth our while to return for a moment to the text of Mr. Frame's essay in order that we may attempt a hypothetical reconstruction of this battle with words.

Let us suppose that we have duplicated Mr. Frame's preparatory thinking on the subject of Hamlet's soliloquies and are now ready to write the second paragraph of our essay. We wish to establish the central image of a man in whom mere doubt becomes virulent and lethal under the influences of a too active mind; and we wish to show that this fatal journey towards complete lack of faith, and especially lack of faith in himself, is the chief record of the soliloquies. Let us see how we might arrive at Mr. Frame's first sentence:

The ability to argue on both sides of a question normally implies only an alert and ingenious mind, but this faculty runs riot once a man loses faith in himself, and, once let slip, seems only to intensify his original feeling of inadequacy.

Since most people are able to see two sides of a question without being destroyed, we must begin with a general condition:

The ability to—

To what? *See* both sides of a question? But this is too passive for Hamlet's case, which is the one we are concerned with. What, then, does Hamlet do—*consider, ponder, evaluate* both sides of a question? One of these might serve, but we think of the soliloquies. Hamlet *argues* with himself, it would seem. Very well:

The ability to argue on both sides of a question—

Now for the idea that this ability generally indicates a certain type of mind. *Generally indicates?* Or *generally suggests?* Or *usually implies?* Yes—*usually implies.* But the particular case, which is again Hamlet's, implies an almost pathological condition. For the general case, then, why not *normal?*

The ability to argue on both sides of a question normally implies only—

Some kind of mind. *Active? Lively? Alert? Alert* will do. But an *alert* mind is not necessarily clever; *alertness* emphasizes receiving, *cleverness* emphasizes dispensing. We might therefore try *alert and clever mind.* Yet *clever* is a word with rather mundane associations. What type of mind makes complex observations on life and the nature of man? An *ingenious* mind. So:

The ability to argue on both sides of a question normally implies only an alert and ingenious mind, but—

But this ability runs hog-wild, we mean to say, when a man (Hamlet, for instance) loses faith in himself. Is it quite right, however, to say that an ability runs wild, and do we in any case want to repeat the word? Why not the *faculty* (of reason) which stands behind the *ability.* *Faculty,* then. And *runs hog-wild* will hardly do. *Runs wild?* Or shall we try *runs riot* for its more specific and human image? Thus:

The ability to argue on both sides of a question normally implies only an alert and ingenious mind, but this faculty runs riot once a man loses faith in himself—

And what happens once this faculty runs riot? We want a sense of cumulative effect, of a bad condition made worse. But it will be cumbersome and repetitious to say that the running riot *increases his sense of loss of faith in himself*; and in any event *loses faith* suggests an absolute condition. We shall have to shift the phrasing here. Loss of faith speaks of a general *feeling of inadequacy*; and to make clear that this is identifiable with the loss of faith which made the faculty run riot, we must say *original feeling of inadequacy*. Now for the thought of aggravation. *Aggravates? Renders worse? Heightens? Deepens? Intensifies? Renders worse* is an ill phrase, but any of the others will do. *Intensifies* is particularly good—it suggests *tension*, a word appropriate to Hamlet's case. We are ready to finish the sentence.

The ability to argue on both sides of a question normally implies only an alert and ingenious mind, but this faculty runs riot once a man loses faith in himself, and seems only to intensify his original feeling of inadequacy.

But we have forgotten that the phrase *this faculty runs riot* must find an echo in the latter part of the sentence if the time sequence is to be kept clear. The *original feeling of inadequacy* is intensified once this faculty *is turned loose* (to suggest the idea of running riot, without repetition). The phrase *runs riot*, however, seems to stir an association in our minds. Is it Antony's "Cry 'Havoc' and let slip the dogs of war"? In any case, *let slip* is more concrete visually than *let loose*, and has the added advantage of suggesting a declension—appropriate again to Hamlet's particular case. Therefore:

The ability to argue on both sides of a question normally implies only an alert and ingenious mind, but this faculty runs riot once a man loses faith in himself, and, once let slip, seems only to intensify his original feeling of inadequacy.

Exaggeration is inevitable when certain almost instantaneous perceptions of the mind are held back to a slower mode of consciousness. In any event, it is clear that this reconstruction of the processes involved in choosing the key words for a single sentence is hypothetical. No doubt the problems of diction just represented differ in many ways from those which Mr. Frame actually faced in writing this sentence; and it is quite probable that Mr. Frame chose without hesitation some of the key words over which we have laboured. Nevertheless, as already suggested, diction is choice, and all choice involves second thought, even if that second thought is so sure and so swift as to be almost instinctive. The analysis provided, therefore, illustrates accurately the essential characteristics of good work in diction. Further illustration could of course be drawn from almost any other sentence in Mr. Frame's essay, as indeed it could be drawn from almost any sentence printed in this book. The student will be well advised to try his hand at this kind of exercise. He will stand to learn much, for example, from watching Professor Knox at work choosing words. He has only to play intelligently the game of question and answer:

Question: In an essay on recent Shakespearean criticism, how am I to represent briefly the work that has been done on the play texts— work that deals with how the texts have been passed on through the centuries, with what relation our present texts bear to the manuscripts, now lost, that came from Shakespeare's hands, with the correcting of printers' errors and the emending of readings, and with the fixing of the probable order in which Shakespeare's plays were written?

Answer: . . . the work on the play texts, on the problems of *transmission, authenticity, revision,* and *chronology.*

Question: If E. K. Chambers discussed the views of various critics in his two-volume *William Shakespeare,* did he also *bring them together, itemize them, list them, outline them, identify them, present them, summarize them, advance them, propound them, expound them, synopsize them,* or *render them?*

Answer: . . . and in 1930 their views were *summarized* and discussed by Chambers in the two volumes of his *William Shakespeare.*

A few further comments are necessary to emphasize three aspects of the general problem of diction which have been only hinted at in the foregoing discussion. These are: first, the question of what may be called momentum in writing; second, the question of substitute or "echo" words and phrases; and third, the question of metaphor.

The question of momentum is suggested by the complexity of the analysis to which a single sentence of Mr. Frame's essay has been subjected. If there are to be eight key words in a sentence, it may be asked, and if a final choice in each case entails reviewing the qualifications of a dozen competing expressions, will the sentence ever be written? Or, if it is written, will it not be written so ponderously that the effect of a vigorous flow of ideas, which we

recognize as an attribute of good writing, is lost? To some extent
these fears are removed when we remind ourselves that the method
of analysis attempted is necessarily laborious and also that increasing
skill in diction brings such resourcefulness and such prompt decisions
about words that no serious impediments are likely to occur. Yet the
need for maintaining momentum remains, and the danger which the
student faces of bogging down in a worried search for words is a
real one. It must simply be said, then, that this search should never
so usurp the writer's attention that the larger movements of thought
on which the essay's argument depends are made to falter, and so
lose their force. Conscientiousness carried this far ceases to be a
virtue. In fact the tendency to give inordinate attention to diction in
the first draft of an essay may well be a danger signal pointing to the
writer's inadequate grasp of his subject; and in so far as this is the
case he will be better advised to reconsider his whole argument than
to continue to wrestle with the choosing of a handful of words.
When he returns to his writing he may find that many apparent
difficulties have disappeared. But if he still has trouble with a
particular passage he will be wise to push on anyway. A word or a
phrase is a thought, and one thought is a breeder of other and
perhaps better thoughts. Thus he may benefit from the flow
developed. At the same time, he must recognize that this solution
accentuates the importance of revision. Examining his completed
first draft, he must ask himself whether this or that word is as
serviceable in its context as some other word might be. Even the
experienced writer will make many changes at this point, and it is
fair to say that any writer will find the reconsideration of diction at
once the most demanding and the most rewarding of the activities
of revision.

One of the graces of a rich language is that approximately the
same thing can be said in many different ways, and the student will
discover that he has to draw constantly upon these resources for a
supply of words and phrases which will be substitutes for, or which
will in some way echo, ideas previously expressed. These variants
serve to protect the reader's ear from the clang of repeated verbal
sounds. More significantly, they are both a cohesive force which helps
to bind together the parts of a unit of argument and an important
means of clarifying and expanding the reader's grasp of a given idea.
In the present paragraph, the phrase *a supply of words and phrases*

which will be substitutes for, or which will in some way echo, ideas previously expressed is a full and formal statement of the topic to be discussed. When this topic is pursued in the sentence which follows, however, the word *variant* replaces the definition already given. Repetition is thereby avoided, and an important link provided in the paragraph's sequence of ideas. At the same time, the reader's understanding of the topic is confirmed and clarified. Examples of this procedure abound in the specimen essays printed in this book. We have already seen that Mr. Frame resorts to variant wordings three times within the short compass of the sentence analysed above; and elsewhere in his essay Hamlet's *hypercritical attitude toward himself* becomes in turn his *suspicion of his own motives*, his *uncharitable view of his own motives*, his *self-contempt*, his *deep-seated distrust of his own motives*, his *self-recrimination*, his *ever-present distrust of himself*, and his *fancied inadequacies*. Elsewhere again, Hamlet's *tardy revenge* becomes *the delay*; and Polonius becomes, at a second point of reference in the same sentence, the *old schemer*. Further examples can be found in Professor Knox's essay. Thus:

Pollard, Chambers, McKerrow, Greg, etc.	becomes	*these textual scholars*
the stress . . . on the mediaeval element in Elizabethan thought	becomes	*the theme* of a certain book
the dramatic and theatrical conventions which were accepted by the Elizabethans	becomes	*the survival of primitive techniques*
the tendency to lose sight of the drama as that presents the characters and actions of men	becomes	*that danger*

By finding accurate and illuminating equivalents for thoughts already broached, or about to be broached, the writer facilitates transitions of thought throughout his essay; more profoundly, he provides an intricate network of internal allusion which will constantly reinforce the import of his argument.

Finally, there is the relation of metaphor to the general problem of diction; and what is to be emphasized here is that the choice of the right word is often the choice of an essentially metaphorical one. A. J. M. Smith in his "The Refining Fire" defines poetry as "a highly organized, complex, and unified re-creation of experience in which the maximum use of meaning and suggestion in the sounds of words has been achieved with the minimum essential outlay of words." There is nothing to prevent the writer of prose from making use, with a difference of degree only, of the same efficient and suggestive means of expression as form the chief stock-in-trade of the poet. And efficiency and suggestiveness in communication point unmistakably to metaphor. This is not to be construed as sanction for pretentious use of imagery in the essay. But it is a recommendation to the writer to consider in his choice of words the power of metaphorical usage to sharpen and extend the reader's understanding of a complex idea by presenting him with an image drawn from the world of sensory experience. Mr. Frame, for example, although he writes a sober enough prose, draws frequently on the resources of metaphor. On one occasion he says of Hamlet that *the sands of his values are already shifting;* on another, that *he attempts to lash himself into the fury he thinks he should feel;* on another (less happily), *that his powers of decision are trammelled . . . in a cloud of brittle logic;* on another, *that his constant questioning has not pierced the veil of doubt that envelops him, but has merely turned a harsher light upon his own fancied inadequacies;* on another, that he is aware that Rosencrantz and Guildenstern *are parrying his plans for revenge;* and, in the final paragraph, that *this is the study of a man struggling in a mire of doubt.* Similarly, in Professor Knox's essay we read that textual scholars have *frowned* upon J. M. Robertson, that Bradley's *Shakespearean Tragedy* has been considered the *Shakespeare student's bible,* that E. E. Stoll brings a *healthy corrective* to excessive concern for characterization, that the English history plays can be seen as *mirrors* of Elizabethan policy, that A. Harbage likes *to poke fun* at certain types of criticism. These are clear, even obvious examples. Beyond them, of course, lie many instances of nearly metaphorical usage (as when Professor Knox records that early in the century *a brilliant band of scholars* gave a *new lead* to criticism) in which the connotative and associative values inherent in most words create at least the hint of a concrete image. But whatever the degree of metaphorical suggestion, the principle remains the same: language kept under a desirable state of tension —"the maximum use of meaning and suggestion . . . achieved with the minimum essential outlay of words." What is to be added is only the reminder that this principle is a continuing challenge to the highest skills of the writer. On the one hand, there is the need for freshness, since trite metaphor deadens rather than vitalizes an idea; and we may note that this is a need not wholly met by Mr. Frame's *shifting sands* and *veil of doubt*. On the other, there is the need for consistency and appropriateness—a need met when Professor Knox's *doctors* are given *instruments* (rather than tools), but dubiously satisfied in Mr. Frame's *cloud of brittle logic*, or in his *mire of doubt*, which too soon becomes an *ocean of disbelief*. Metaphorical usage is desirable; but metaphorical usage is good usage only when it is the mark of expert craftsmanship.

This discussion has analysed the problem of diction and adduced the more important principles involved in the precise, appropriate, and resourceful use of words. But about the tremendous and fundamental problem of how the student is to build and gain control over a complex vocabulary it has had little specifically to say. The fact is that there is very little indeed that can be said on this score—and very much that must be done by the student himself. Behind the skilful writer's use of words lie both a lifetime of extensive reading, in the course of which he has observed words at work in a multitude of combinations and in a multitude of contexts, and doubtless years of practice in handling the counters of language. Obviously the student cannot acquire this kind of equipment simply by clapping hand to brow and resolving to improve the diction of his next essay. Yet he can and must begin to strengthen a basic weakness, where a basic weakness exists. In particular, as the experienced writer has done, he must read widely and practise constantly the art of writing. And if he considers carefully and applies to the analysis of both his reading and his writing the principles discussed in the preceding pages; if he listens intelligently to the more routine forms of good advice for the novice which tell him to prefer the concrete word to the abstract, the familiar word to the far-fetched, and the short word to the long—which tell him in sum to be direct, simple, brief, vigorous, and lucid before he is anything else; if he discovers what a good dictionary can do for him and what it cannot do for him, and learns of the great amount of help with words he can secure from dictionaries of synonyms and antonyms and from such special compilations as Roget's *Thesaurus* and H. W. Fowler's *The King's English* and *Modern English Usage*—if he does all these things he may expect to make heartening gains. His reward will be not only better marks but the satisfaction which comes from a growing command over the chief instruments of his intelligence.

Punctuation

ALL COMPOSITION HANDBOOKS treat punctuation in essentially the same way. The rules which govern the use of each of the punctuation marks are listed, and the errors which would result should these rules not be observed are identified and deplored. The information thus provided enables the writer to determine whether his punctuation in a given sentence is acceptable or not. What the handbooks seldom do, however, is to explain what punctuation is and what ends it serves. Consequently they disappoint the student who seeks a statement of principles which will enable him to see the listed rules not as isolated phenomena, but as related units in a rational system. This chapter attempts such a statement; by seeking an answer to the question "What is punctuation?" it reveals the logical pattern which underlies the rules.

Punctuation marks are signals. They enable the writer to indicate to the reader how a passage is to be read. If the writer could not be sure that his reader assigned one value to a period, another and quite different value to a comma, he would be powerless to control the reader's progress across the page. But the writer can control the reader's progress, for, consciously or unconsciously, the reader does respond in a definite and predictable fashion not only to the appearance of the period and the comma but to the appearance of the other marks as well. To take advantage of this situation, the writer obviously must know exactly what the reader's response to each punctuation mark will be.

The most satisfactory method of discovering the predictable responses of the reader is to study the way in which punctuation marks are used by writers whose standards are currently respected. It is a historical fact that the rules of punctuation—which are simply the codification of conventional practice at a given time—have been subject to revision over the centuries; for this reason, Sir Winston Churchill and T. S. Eliot furnish a sounder model for the writer of today than do Sir Philip Sidney and William Shakespeare, whose punctuation reflects the practice of Englishmen writing 350 years ago. Churchill and Eliot have had to adapt their practice to the habitual responses of twentieth-century readers, as have the authors of the essays printed in Part I of this book.

One of the principal functions of punctuation does not require comment in a book entitled *The Undergraduate Essay*. Every undergraduate knows that the nature of a sentence—whether statement, question, or exclamation—is indicated by the punctuation mark placed at the end of the sentence. We shall confine our attention to two other important functions which, though similar in purpose, can most satisfactorily be treated separately. The first is the use of punctuation to distinguish the main ideas from each other and to indicate their relationship. The second is the use of punctuation to make clear the identity of the main ideas by marking off sentence elements which are non-restrictive or parenthetical, that is, elements which can be detached from the sentence without affecting the essential meaning of the sentence. The first of these functions involves the use of period, colon, semicolon, and comma. The second involves the use of commas, dashes, and parentheses (round brackets).

I. The Identification and Relation of Main Ideas

We sometimes forget how heavily we rely on punctuation marks to direct our path through a landscape of words:

from time to time new diseases make their appearance some are attributable to social or scientific progress to contact with new products of chemical industry or adventure into new physical conditions in others the origin is obscure the latest of these is of a particularly distressing kind it is a form of blindness in both eyes practically confined to premature babies from its main characteristic the formation of fibrous or scar tissue behind the lens it is called retrolental fibroplasia from this tissue strands extend across the interior of the eyeball to the retina and these on contracting cause retinal detachment in labelling a disease new caution is needed some diseases are new only in the sense that new methods of diagnosis or treatment bring them to light the classical example is appendicitis others are merely pre-existing diseases separated out from an ill-defined group by better understanding of their nature retrolental fibroplasia belongs in neither of these categories since the eye by virtue of its transparency lends itself uniquely to direct examination by means of the ophthalmoscope an instrument which has been in use for many years it is inconceivable that the previous existence of this condition could have been overlooked it is without doubt a new disease

Presented without benefit of punctuation marks, these first 200 words of "A New Disease" are very difficult to unravel. Much of the difficulty arises from the absence of easily recognized sentences and paragraphs. The *look* of a sentence signals something to us—that the words thus associated produce in combination what we may call a sentence-idea. (As we shall see, the sentence-idea may contain within itself two or more distinct ideas; however, a single idea emerges from such a sentence, a new idea which embraces the separate ideas and over-rides their potential self-sufficiency.) Similarly, the *look* of a paragraph signals something to us—that the sentences thus associated produce in combination a paragraph-idea. Punctuation facilitates written communication by defining the functional units of thought.

Though we do not normally think of paragraph indentation as a form of punctuation, we are justified in including it in our discussion since it is the conventional device for signalling the limits of a paragraph. "A paragraph is a group of sentences designed to develop a single unit of thought" (page 57). Certainly this is a more satisfactory definition of the paragraph than "a group of sentences standing between two paragraph indentations." Yet it is the indentation that alerts the reader to the fact that what follows is "a group of sentences designed to develop a single unit of thought." Likewise, though we shall not be satisfied with defining the sentence as "a group of words, the first of which begins with a capital letter and the last of which is followed by either a period, a question mark, or an exclamation mark," we must recognize that it is punctuation which provides the physical evidence for identifying the unit of thought we call the sentence.

Here is Dr. Roberts' first paragraph reproduced with *sentence* punctuation, and with paragraph indentation added (indentation is not customary in opening paragraphs):

From time to time new diseases make their appearance. Some are attributable to social or scientific progress to contact with new products of chemical industry or adventure into new physical conditions. In others the origin is obscure. The latest of these is of a particularly distressing kind. It is a form of blindness in both eyes practically confined to premature babies. From its main characteristic the formation of fibrous or scar tissue behind the lens it is called retrolental fibroplasia. From this tissue strands extend across the interior of the eyeball to the retina and these on contracting cause retinal detachment.

The passage now contains only minor difficulties, for, since the successive ideas are presented in sentence units, we are able to proceed without confusion from one idea to the next. As we study the passage, we note that, except in the final sentence, a single idea is presented in each sentence. The final sentence contains two ideas which merge into a single sentence-idea, a compounding which is signalled by the placing of a comma at the point of juncture:

From this tissue strands extend across the interior of the eyeball, and these on contracting cause retinal detachment.

The third paragraph of Mr. Henn's "The Canadian Dilemma," though twice the length of Dr. Roberts' opening paragraph, contains only four sentences. Of these, the last occupies as much space as Dr. Roberts' seven sentences:

The explanation of why this possibility has not been realized is to be found in two additional circumstances: first, Canada is still in the initial stage of a long-term boom, and her population is as yet far too small to make large-scale mass production and nationwide distribution-networks feasible; secondly, and perhaps more important, the Dominion Government has imposed a heavy scheme of taxation in order to finance a welfare programme which many people feel to be more ambitious than a nation of this size can afford without crippling, or at least inhibiting, its development in the immediate future.

This, though long, is not a confusing sentence, for the writer has welded the several distinct ideas contained in the sentence into a unified whole (or sentence-idea) by his use of three punctuation marks. He knows that the reader can be expected to respond differently to a colon, a semicolon and a comma, and he indicates the relation of the separate ideas in the sentence by employing these marks. The sentence can be said to contain four independent statements, each capable of being expressed in a complete sentence:

1. The explanation of why this possibility has not been realized is to be found in two additional circumstances.
2. Canada is still in the initial stage of a long-term boom.
3. Her population is as yet far too small to make large-scale mass production and nationwide distribution-networks feasible.
4. The Dominion Government has imposed a heavy scheme of taxation in order to finance a welfare programme which many people feel to be more ambitious than a nation of this size can afford without crippling, or at least inhibiting, its development in the immediate future.

Yet these four ideas have different degrees of importance. Statement 1 can be said to embrace Statements 2, 3, and 4, since these statements identify the "two additional circumstances" which explain "why this possibility has not been realized." One of these circumstances is presented in Statements 2 and 3, the second in Statement 4. In relative importance, then, Statement 4 is the equivalent of Statements 2 *and* 3, while, in parallel to the combination of Statements 2 and 3, it is subordinate to Statement 1:

Statement 1   embraces   { $\dfrac{\text{Statement 2}\quad\text{and}\quad\text{Statement 3}}{\substack{\text{in parallel to}\\ \text{Statement 4}}}$

Mr. Henn indicates this complex of relations by assuming that the reader will give heavy weight to the colon, medium weight to the semicolon, and light weight to the comma:

(1) COLON   embraces   { $\dfrac{\text{(2) COMMA}\quad\text{and}\quad\text{(3) SEMICOLON}}{\text{(4)}\qquad\qquad\text{SEMICOLON}}$

Since Statement 4 concludes the sentence, the semicolon placed at the end of (4) above is replaced by a period. Light punctuation marks always yield to heavy punctuation marks; except when parentheses are involved, we never place two punctuation marks side by side. Henn makes the same assumptions to solve a similar problem in the second sentence of his fifth paragraph: here he relates four ideas, three of which are embraced by the first. The formula is

(1) COLON   embraces   { $\begin{array}{ll} \text{(2)} & \text{SEMICOLON} \\ \hline \text{(3)} & \text{SEMICOLON} \\ \hline \text{(4)} & \text{SEMICOLON (PERIOD)} \end{array}$

When two ideas are drawn together into a single sentence-idea, the comma and the semicolon are the conventional means of signalling co-ordination or subordination. Given two distinct ideas, various combinations of co-ordination and subordination are possible. Here is the first sentence of Mr. Henn's third paragraph as he has written it (Version 1) and as he might have written it. (The new versions should not be regarded as model sentences; they are presented here solely to illustrate certain principles of punctuation.) In Versions 1, 2, and 3 the ideas are co-ordinated, that is, given equal logical status; in Versions 4 and 5 one of the ideas is subordinated to the other:

1. Canadians have a painfully simple reason for being envious; the fact is that virtually everything requiring an outlay of money, from cigarettes to gasoline, from railroad fares to rents, is cheaper in the United States.

2. Canadians have a painfully simple reason for being envious. The fact is that virtually everything requiring an outlay of money, from cigarettes to gasoline, from railroad fares to rents, is cheaper in the United States.

3. Canadians have a painfully simple reason for being envious, for virtually everything requiring an outlay of money, from cigarettes to gasoline, from railroad fares to rents, is cheaper in the United States.

4. Canadians have a painfully simple reason for being envious because everything requiring an outlay of money, from cigarettes to gasoline, from railroad fares to rents, is cheaper in the United States.

5. As virtually everything requiring an outlay of money, from cigarettes to gasoline, from railroad fares to rents, is cheaper in the United States, Canadians have a painfully simple reason for being envious.

Though the ideas are co-ordinated in each of the first three versions, the response of the reader varies with the punctuation used. When the two ideas are placed in separate sentences (Version 2), they are co-ordinated only in the sense that they both enjoy the status of complete sentence and they are juxtaposed; the period emphasizes their independence, and the reader receives the ideas as a sequence. When the ideas are related by the semicolon, a medium-weight stop, the reader receives the ideas as a combination; independence and interdependence are jointly asserted (Version 1). When the ideas are related by a comma (working in co-operation with the co-ordinate conjunction *for*), the emphasis is on interdependence (Version 3).

Subordination is achieved in Versions 4 and 5 by the use of one of the subordinating conjunctions (*because, as*), which need to be carefully distinguished from the co-ordinating conjunctions (*and, but, for, so, or, nor*). These two sentences illustrate the normal method of punctuating sentences containing one main and one subordinate clause; where the subordinate clause precedes the main clause (Version 5), a comma is placed at their juncture; the comma usually does not appear when the subordinate clause follows the main clause (Version 4). Compare Version 4 with the following:

6. Because virtually everything requiring an outlay of money, from cigarettes to gasoline, from railroad fares to rents, is cheaper in the United States, Canadians have a painfully simple reason for being envious.

It is also possible to express Mr. Henn's sentence-idea as a single direct statement:

7. The fact that virtually everything requiring an outlay of money, from cigarettes to gasoline, from railroad fares to rents, is cheaper in the United States provides a painfully simple reason why Canadians are envious.

Here there is no punctuation to indicate the co-existence of two distinct ideas for the simple reason that only one idea is presented. The phrasing has submerged the identity of the two ideas in a single statement: *The fact that virtually everything requiring an outlay of money is cheaper in the United States provides a painfully simple reason why Canadians are envious.* We have no more reason to employ punctuation here than we have in the sentence, *The dog bites the cat.*

II. The Identification of Non-Restrictive Material

The second function of punctuation which we are concerned with is its use to identify parenthetical or non-restrictive material, material which can be removed from the sentence without affecting the essential meaning of the sentence. Parenthetical material is normally enclosed within a pair of punctuation marks—commas, dashes, or parentheses; but, as we shall see, one of the pair of enclosing marks is sometimes missing. We have encountered instances of parenthetical material in the sentences and paragraphs already examined—for example, the phrases "from cigarettes to gasoline" and "from railroad fares to rents" in Mr. Henn's much revised sentence.

The distinction between restrictive and non-restrictive material can be seen in the first sentence of Professor Knox's final paragraph:

The prevalent concern in the most recent criticism, *as this survey has tried to show,* has been with the imagery and symbolism of the plays, *with the plays, one might almost say, as dramatic poems*; and few would deny the further reaches of Shakespeare's art which have thus been opened.

The non-restrictive material has been italicized. If this material were removed, the sentence would retain its essential meaning:

The prevalent concern in the most recent criticism has been with the imagery and symbolism of the plays; and few would deny the further reaches of Shakespeare's art which have thus been opened.

In saying that the removal of non-restrictive material does not affect the sentence's essential meaning, we are, of course, on slippery ground; all elements in the sentence contribute to its meaning. Yet there is a difference between the essential and the merely helpful. The clause, *as this survey has tried to show,* places the statement in context by referring back to the preceding paragraphs. The phrase, *with the plays as dramatic poems,* is even more helpful, for, by restating in a different way the idea contained in *with the imagery and symbolism of the plays,* it expands and enriches the original. The clause, *one might almost say,* is a helpful little aside, one which gives emphasis to *with the plays as dramatic poems* and which contributes to the rhythm of the sentence. But none of this is essential. In contrast, the final clause of the sentence, *which have thus been opened,* is essential (restrictive), for if it is omitted the sentence ceases to make sense:

The prevalent concern in the most recent criticism, as this survey has tried to show, has been with the imagery and symbolism of the plays, with the plays, one might almost say, as dramatic poems; and few would deny the further reaches of Shakespeare's art.

The clause, *which have thus been opened,* is a restrictive clause, one which cannot be removed without sacrificing essential meaning. The absence of a comma before *which* is, paradoxically, a signal that what follows is restrictive.

Of the three instances of non-restrictive material in Professor Knox's sentence, two are enclosed within commas: *as this survey has tried to show* and *one might almost say.* The third, *with the plays as dramatic poems,* is introduced by a comma, but the expected concluding comma does not appear because it must yield place to the semicolon which the structure of the sentence demands at this point for other reasons. The introductory comma is missing when the non-restrictive material appears at the beginning of the sentence:

Fortunately, the period under review has been as distinguished in its Shakespearean productions as in its criticism.

Here is the remainder of Professor Knox's final paragraph, with the non-restrictive material italicized:

But great art such as Shakespeare's has many related aspects. In our concern with the poetry we may have tended to lose sight of the drama as that presents the characters and actions of men. That danger the theatre itself can best avert; and for a full appreciation of the play criticism must always take second place to what is gained by the vivid life of the stage. *Fortunately,* the period under review has been as distinguished in its Shakespearean productions as in its criticism. *Indeed,* one of the best of the period's critics, *H. Granville-Barker,* was both producer and actor, and in his *Prefaces to Shakespeare's Plays* he has brilliantly demonstrated his twofold gift of revealing the subtleties of the dramatist's art, *especially in character creation,* and of showing how best the plays can be fitted to the theatre. He and William Poel, *his teacher,* were the modern pioneers in giving us the plays practically as they were written, *with the minimum of cuts and with no unwarranted elaborations.* Their lead has since been worthily followed, and today, *in the best productions of London's Old Vic or Canada's Stratford,* we have Shakespeare probably more authentically with us than at any time since the seventeenth century.

Throughout, commas are employed to set off the non-restrictive material—the normal method. A somewhat different effect would have resulted if Professor Knox had used dashes and brackets:

Indeed, one of the best of the period's critics (H. Granville-Barker) was both producer and actor, and in his *Prefaces to Shakespeare's Plays* he has brilliantly demonstrated his twofold gift of revealing the subtleties of the dramatist's art, especially in character creation, and of showing how best the plays can be fitted to the theatre. He and William Poel, his teacher, were the modern pioneers in giving us the plays practically as they were written—with the minimum of cuts and with no unwarranted elaborations. Their lead. . . .

The question of when to use dashes and brackets in place of commas is almost entirely a matter of taste: there are no unbreakable rules. Yet—and this we can verify by comparing this revised version with the original—the effect of dashes is different than the effect of commas and the effect of brackets is different than that of either commas or dashes. Dashes give increased emphasis—*with the minimum of cuts and with no unwarranted elaborations* stands out more clearly on the page in the revised version and we read it with more attention. Brackets tend to isolate the material contained within them (their physical prominence tends to detach their content from the content of the sentence itself); in the revised version *H. Granville-Barker* happens to be the critic named; we ought to know this, but the important point is that "one of the best of the period's critics was both producer and actor." Most writers employ the dash principally to obtain a striking effect and the bracket to interject casual comment or to provide definition or explanation. Obviously, for maximum effect both should be used judiciously. One can cry "Wolf" only a certain number of times. The student should decide for himself the precise effect his dashes and brackets are intended to convey, and this he can most satisfactorily do by examining the use of these punctuation marks by such writers as Henn, Smith, and Winch.

CONCLUSION

"Punctuation marks are signals. They permit the writer to indicate to the reader how a passage is to be read." Like fences which mark the boundaries of fields, punctuation marks define the boundaries of units of thought, whether major (cf. Section I) or minor (cf. Section II). Sensible men do not erect fences without a purpose in mind. Sensible writers do not use punctuation marks unless they have a purpose in mind. There are reasons enough for using punctuation marks, as these pages have shown. If the writer constantly keeps in mind that his punctuation marks are signals which elicit a definite response from his reader, the mysteries of this subject vanish and are replaced by mere problems of procedure.

The Conventions of Scholarship

IN OUR LETTERS to our friends and relations we follow certain conventions automatically, forgetting that long ago we had to learn how and when to use them. If we examine these conventions, we find that they have a *rationale*: beginning one letter "Dear John" and a second "My dear Harry," we indicate thereby a subtle difference in our relation to the two correspondents, a distinction we make again when we conclude in one case with "Yours sincerely" and in the second with "Yours." Some of the conventions are typographical: for example, we write our address and the date in a particular place on a particular page. The conventions which we observe in letter writing are principally designed to improve the appearance of the page or to place important information in a prominent position.

Scholarly writing also has its conventions, and these we must master if we wish to function effectively in the world of scholarship, whether as writers or readers. The conventions of scholarly writing are all designed to facilitate communication; they are not barriers maliciously erected to keep out undesirables. Their purpose is either to make the reader's task simpler and more pleasant or to provide information about the writer's source material which will enable the reader to investigate the subject further on his own.

Since the undergraduate essay is a scholarly work in miniature, these conventions are our direct concern. They are fully described in *Scholarly Reporting in the Humanities*, a fifty-page pamphlet prepared for the Humanities Research Council of Canada, which is designed primarily for the scholar who is preparing a manuscript for publication either as a book or as an article in a learned journal; it contains, therefore, much more information than is needed by the student who is preparing an undergraduate essay for submission to his instructor. Comparable information is provided in *A Manual for the Writers of Term Papers, Theses, and Dissertations* by Kate L. Turabian (Chicago: University of Chicago Press, 1955). The following remarks on the appearance of the manuscript, on the use of primary and secondary sources, on the form of footnotes and on the preparation of a bibliography are restricted to matters which are certain to be of concern to the undergraduate.

(Specimen Page)

THE TITLE IN CAPITALS (1)

Yos biw us tge trne fir skk uuddk neb ti xxine ti tge audkkdk idh (2)

ieicmlle. Swwm idllye xiu cieuel form eiwowox, ieiemlle losopw iek (3)

to elwo idme. Miei lisiem iie di wiqo rros seitme losie, con formedi

sleo.

Yiosp diead ieeks lowl id eiei eieow, wiile ieisl eielssl lows ro (4)

timel. Idkelos ieis ford lowis, posiwl ieds lso wqq ratomeis osped

so brilliantly expressed by W. B. Yeats: (5)

O chestnut tree, great rooted blossomer, (6)
Are you the leaf, the blossom or the bole?
O body swayed to music, O brightening glance,
How can we know the dancer from the dance?

("Among School Children," 53-56) (7)

Islw uuel uf ieksl siskekdkel a ies sim, for soomecid odieu du soeklwid,

foroed ti oel. Skeielsl die, eeedk, ed ieekslsoe od und immedkiil

idkeieys:

The opposition of life and death forces is strong in Macbeth. Here we (8)
find the dark and evil negation endued with a positive strength, success-
fully opposing things of health and life. ... In Hamlet, we find the same (9) (10)
opposition,.... [In it] life forces are vividly and very clearly contrasted (11)
with evil.[1]

Uieye emdl ididl eidiwls, anddy eme orime form simce. Ikse eemdu

eis ie liisle. Wowe, ieiem leoisdies idoslel fueeud lsoeld. Ord, as

Knight has also said, "these are typical Shakespearean themes."[2] Iuuyr (12)

isu uu curidls ienhelseldil. Illiel didil eieieslei w mieiosl form: "Thou (13)

sure and firm-set earth/ Hear not my steps" (II, i, 52-53). Oydis osoei die,

iiels ford idlwso llsos eiwoslg idislw.[3] Oodoolsle iowos, cowidlgei (14)

(15)

(16)

---

1. Knight, Imperial Theme, 125.
2. Ibid., 126.
3. See Bradley, Shakespearean Tragedy, vii, and, for a more detailed
analysis, MacLure, "Shakespeare and the Lonely Dragon," 109-20.

(1) The first page of the essay is not numbered since the title occupies the central position at the head of the page. Arabic numerals are used thereafter.

(2) The first paragraph of the essay is not indented.

(3) The lines of the essay are double-spaced in contrast to quoted material which, when off-set, is single-spaced. See Notes 6 and 8, but also 12 and 13, below.

(4) The second and succeeding paragraphs are given paragraph indentation (five spaces on the typewriter).

(5) Quotations are normally introduced by a colon.

(6) A verse quotation of more than one line is set off from the main body of the essay. It is centred on the page. The quotation is single-spaced. It is not enclosed in quotation marks. The lines may be identified by a footnote or (as here) in a parenthesis placed to the right of the final line quoted.

(7) The title of a poem is enclosed in quotation marks.

(8) A prose quotation of three lines or more is set off from the essay proper but, unlike the verse quotation, is given the same left-hand margin as the main text. It is single-spaced. Quotation marks are not used. The quotation is identified by a footnote.

(9) If one or more words are omitted from a quotation (prose or verse), the omission is recognized by an ellipsis (3 dots). If the ellipsis follows a completed sentence, the three dots will be preceded by a space and a period ("health and life. ..."). If the ellipsis includes the latter part of a sentence, the three dots will be followed by a period ("the same opposition. . . .").

(10) The title of a published work (play, novel, collection of poems) is italicized (underlined). See Note 7 above.

(11) Any word or words inserted by the writer of the essay within a quotation (for example, to preserve grammatical sense) are enclosed in square brackets.

(12) A prose quotation occupying less than three lines is normally incorporated in the text and enclosed by quotation marks. The quotation is identified by a footnote. A sentence which incorporates a quotation (prose or verse) must remain a grammatical sentence.

(13) A verse quotation of less than two complete lines may be incorporated in the text, in which case it is enclosed in quotation marks. A virgule (/) is inserted to mark the end of the poetic line. All capital letters in the original are retained. The quotation can be identified in a parenthesis.

(14) A footnote reference can be used for other purposes than the identification of quotations.

(15) A line drawn across the page conveniently separates body of text from footnotes.

(16) The footnotes here are given at the bottom of the page. Alternatively, they may be placed (as end notes) at the end of the essay, in which case they are numbered consecutively without regard for the page on which they appear.

THE APPEARANCE OF THE MANUSCRIPT

We have seen (p. 65) that a grammatical error is a barrier to effective communication chiefly because it creates doubt in the reader's mind about the qualifications of the writer to speak as an authority on the subject under discussion. A carelessly prepared manuscript creates the same kind of doubt. If the writer has chosen the wrong kind of paper, has failed to provide adequate margins, has not numbered his pages, or has neglected to place the title of the essay in the appropriate position on the first page, the reader is likely to feel either that the writer is ignorant of what constitutes a well-prepared page or that he is not willing to take the necessary pains. To antagonize the reader at the outset is certainly not going to improve our chances of convincing him that what we have to say is sound. But there is a second reason for observing the scholarly conventions; they simplify the reader's task as he reads the essay by making it easy for him to recognize and to identify the evidence which the writer has drawn from his sources to support his argument. The most common conventions are illustrated on page 98 and explained on page 99.

PRIMARY AND SECONDARY SOURCES

The topics set for undergraduate essays normally require the writer to consult both primary and secondary sources. The primary source for Mr. Frame's essay on *Hamlet* is the text of the play: in theory, all the variant texts of this play which have come down to us from Shakespeare's day; in practice, a particular edition—that of Kittredge. The secondary sources theoretically available to him include all books and articles bearing on *Hamlet* written in any language since 1601. For Professor Knox's essay on recent Shakespearean criticism, the primary sources are the books which have been written about Shakespeare's dramatic works during a specified period of time. Secondary sources for this topic include other surveys of "recent Shakespearean criticism," studies of other kinds of "recent" literary criticism, and histories of literary criticism. It is to be noted that both Mr. Frame and Professor Knox refer frequently to primary sources, though seldom to secondary sources.

Since the primary sources are by definition what the essay is about, no scholarly work can avoid them. It is, however, possible to write intelligently and honestly about Hamlet's soliloquies or about recent Shakespearean criticism without referring directly to the text (or texts). The advantages of direct reference are twofold. First, direct quotation is often the most effective method of making a point. Poetry is notoriously difficult to paraphrase, and a writer may waste five lines of prose in rendering what is more clearly said by the poet in the two lines of the original. Second, the appearance of frequent but judiciously selected quotations from the text suggests to the reader that the writer has a firm control over his material. "If he knows his text so well that he can produce a two-line quotation to climax each stage of his argument, surely I must follow his argument with attention."

Secondary sources can also be fruitfully cited, but here there is reason for caution. A scholarly work—and we have rightly described the undergraduate essay as a scholarly work in miniature—is a piece of independent work, the result of its author's own reflection on his material. A collection of the views on *Hamlet* of a dozen critics, no matter how reputable, is not an essay; it is merely a collection of critical views on *Hamlet*. If, however, the writer of the essay has a view of *Hamlet* which differs slightly or markedly from the views of other critics, the most effective way to make his position clear may well be to remind his readers of what other writers have said and then to show how and why he differs. It would be surprising if most of us did not often agree with the opinions of the more reputable critics. A. C. Bradley devoted a good part of a long life to the study of Shakespeare's plays; time and time again, we shall find that his mature conclusions give clear expression to our own as yet unarticulated judgments. We are perfectly justified in quoting Bradley in support of our view. Our position is, indeed, stronger if we can show that it is a position shared by a universally respected critic. But Bradley must remain an assistant, not our master. Unless we have thoroughly studied our primary sources, we have failed to establish our own position. The secondary sources are secondary.

In dealing with secondary sources, we must take immense pains to avoid any act of plagiarism. *Plagiarism* is defined in the *American College Dictionary* as "copying or imitating the language, ideas, and thoughts of another author and passing off the same as one's original work." It is the great intellectual sin. Honesty requires that we give credit where credit is due. If Wilson Knight has opened our eyes to the meaning of a particular passage in *Othello*, we must record our debt. If we use his words in reference to the passage, we must indicate that they are a direct quotation. If we paraphrase his thoughts, we are equally obligated to identify the source of our indebtedness. The undergraduate essay is a scholarly work in miniature. Intellectual dishonesty has no place in the world of scholarship.

THE FORM OF FOOTNOTES

Scholarly Reporting in the Humanities lists five purposes for which footnotes are useful:
  (a) to identify quotations;
  (b) to acknowledge indebtedness for words or ideas borrowed;
  (c) to indicate where additional evidence or comment may be found in printed books or other authoritative sources;
  (d) to furnish additional material or discussion which is pertinent (otherwise it should not be mentioned at all) but which would disturb the proportions of the text if included here;
  (e) to refer to other parts of the dissertation itself.
Footnotes can be placed at the bottom of the page on which they appear (as illustrated in the Specimen Page) or at the end of the essay (as illustrated in Professor Knox's essay)—in the latter case, they are called end notes. The former method is the more convenient for the reader, the latter for the printer.

The purpose of identifying source material, whether primary or secondary, is to enable the reader to consult the original if he wishes. Sufficient information must therefore be provided to enable the reader to obtain the original. In the case of a printed book, he needs to know the name of the author, the title of the book, the place where it was published, the name of the publisher, and the year in which the book was published. In the case of an article in a periodical, he needs to know the name of the author, the title of the article, the name of the periodical, the volume in which it appears (a year of issues normally constitutes a volume), and the pages in the volume occupied by the article. As we shall see, proper bibliographical entries provide this information. There is no need to provide detailed information about a book or article referred to in a footnote if the book or article is included in the bibliography which is provided at the end of the essay. Thus if

> BRADLEY, A. C. *Shakespearean Tragedy*. London: Macmillan, 1904.

is listed in the bibliography, then

> Bradley, *Shakespearean Tragedy*, 126.

is a satisfactory footnote to identify a quotation from page 126. The respective entries for a periodical article are:

> MacLURE, M. "Shakespeare and the Lonely Dragon," *University of Toronto Quarterly*, XXIV (Jan. 1955), 109–20.

and

> MacLure, "Shakespeare and the Lonely Dragon," 110.

The conventions of scholarship include certain abbreviations which are intended to reduce effort in the recording of footnotes. Chief of these is the word *ibid.*, an abbreviation of the Latin *ibidem*, meaning *in the same book* or *chapter* or *page*. Hence if two successive footnotes refer to the same page of Bradley's book, the entries are:

> 1. Bradley, *Shakespearean Tragedy*, 116.
> 2. *Ibid.*

If the second note directed the reader to another page of Bradley's book, the footnotes would be:

> 1. Bradley, *Shakespearean Tragedy*, 116.
> 2. *Ibid.*, 118.

Ibid. refers the reader back to the immediately preceding footnote. Two other abbreviations are often employed to refer the reader back to earlier footnote entries: *op. cit.* (*opus citatum*, the work cited) and *loc. cit.* (*locus citatus*, the place cited), referring respectively to books and periodicals. Thus,

> 1. Bradley, *Shakespearean Tragedy*, vii.
> 2. *Ibid.*, 114.
> 3. MacLure, "Shakespeare and the Lonely Dragon," 109.
> 4. Bradley, *op cit.*, 116.
> 5. MacLure, *loc. cit.*, 110.

There is an increasing tendency to avoid the use of *op. cit.* and *loc. cit.* Little more effort is required to repeat the short titles:

> 4. Bradley, *Shakespearean Tragedy*, 116.
> 5. MacLure, "Shakespeare and the Lonely Dragon," 110.

BIBLIOGRAPHY

It is not necessary in an undergraduate essay or in a scholarly article to list in the bibliography every book or article that the writer has consulted. The list is by implication a selected list; it contains the sources which have been helpful to the writer and which, therefore, are likely to be helpful to the reader who chooses to study the subject further.

The bibliography which appears on page 105 is a list of the works which the authors have found useful in writing this book. It is included primarily to draw attention to works which provide more detailed information about specific aspects of essay writing; for example, Partridge and Clark's *You Have a Point There* is a 200-page treatment of punctuation. The bibliography has the incidental advantage of illustrating the conventional form to be adopted for the various kinds of entry which are likely to find a place in the bibliography of an undergraduate essay: a book by one author (2, 5, 6, etc.), a book by two authors (1, 10), a book written by one author and edited by a second (8), a book that has been anonymously compiled (4, 7, 17), an encyclopaedia reference (13), an article in a learned journal (9), an article in a popular journal (12). The punctuation should be carefully noted. The bibliography follows the approved practice of presenting the entries in alphabetical order.

BIBLIOGRAPHY

1. EVANS, BERGEN and CORNELIA EVANS. *A Dictionary of Contemporary American Usage*. New York: Random House, 1957.
2. FOWLER, H. W. *Dictionary of Modern English Usage*. Oxford: Clarendon Press, 1926.
3. ————and G. F. FOWLER. *The King's English*, 3rd edition. London: Oxford University Press, 1930.
4. Funk and Wagnalls Editorial Staff. *Standard Handbook of Prepositions, Conjunctions, Relative Pronouns, and Adverbs*. New York: Funk and Wagnalls, 1953.
5. GOWERS, SIR ERNEST. *The Complete Plain Words*. London: Her Majesty's Stationery Office, 1954.
6. GRIERSON, HERBERT J. C. *Rhetoric and English Composition*, 2nd edition. Edinburgh: Oliver and Boyd, 1945.
7. Humanities Research Council. *Scholarly Reporting in the Humanities*, 3rd edition. Toronto: University of Toronto Press, 1961.
8. JESPERSEN, OTTO. *A Modern English Grammar on Historical Principles*. 7 vols. Ed. by NIELS HAISLUND. Copenhagen: E. Munsgaard, 1942–9.
9. JOHNSON, ELLEN. "A Simpler Approach to Punctuation," *College English*, XV (April 1954), 399–404.
10. LLOYD, DONALD J. and HARRY R. WERFEL. *American English in its Cultural Setting*. New York: Alfred A. Knopf, 1956.
11. MARCKWARDT, ALBERT H. *American English*. New York: Oxford University Press, 1958.
12. POTTER, C. F. "How Poor are You at Punctuation," *Saturday Evening Post*, April 12, 1947, 49–50, 106–8.
13. "Rhetoric," *Encylopaedia Britannica*, 11th edition.
14. ROBERTS, PAUL. *Understanding Grammar*. New York: Harper & Brothers, 1954.
15. SUTHERLAND, JAMES. *On English Prose*. Toronto: University of Toronto Press, 1957.
16. TURABIAN, KATE L. *A Manual for the Writers of Term Papers, Theses, and Dissertations*, revised edition. Chicago: University of Chicago Press, 1955.
17. *Webster's Dictionary of Synonyms*. Springfield, Mass.: G. and C. Merriam Co., 1942.
18. WHITEHALL, HAROLD. *Structural Essentials of English*. New York: Harcourt Brace, 1951.